AF679397

Mastering REIT Investments - A Comprehensive Guide to Wealth Building

Real Estate Investing, Volume 3

Jim Pellerin

Published by Jim Pellerin, 2024.

MASTERING REIT INVESTMENTS - A COMPREHENSIVE GUIDE TO WEALTH BUILDING

First edition. February 29, 2024.

ISBN: 979-8224376445

Written by Jim Pellerin.

Also by Jim Pellerin

Life Now

Invest Now - The Passive Approach to Winning at Real Estate

Real Estate Investing

Real Estate Investing Strategies: The Secret to Financial Independence with Real Estate
Real Estate Investing with Lease Options - Investing in Real Estate with No Money Down
Mastering REIT Investments - A Comprehensive Guide to Wealth Building
The Ultimate Beginners Guide to Real Estate Investing
The 98 Best Real Estate Investing Strategies
The Ultimate Beginners Guide to Wholesale Real Estate Investing
The Ultimate Beginners Guide to Rental Real Estate Investing
The Ultimate Beginners Guide to Fix and Flip Real Estate Investing
The Ultimate Beginners Guide to Private Equity Real Estate Investing
Ultimate Beginners Guide to Real Estate Investing Financing
Building Wealth Through Real Estate - A Beginners Retirement Guide
The Ultimate Guide to Marketing for Real Estate Investors
Unleashing Wealth: A Guide to BRRRR Real Estate Investing

Watch for more at www.jimpellerin.com.

Table of Contents

Mastering REIT Investments

A Comprehensive Guide to Wealth Building

Jim Pellerin

Updated for 2024

Chapter 1: Introduction to REIT Investing

Real Estate Investment Trusts (REITs) have emerged as a popular and accessible avenue for individuals to participate in the real estate market without the burdens of direct property ownership. In this chapter, we delve into the fundamentals of REIT investing, beginning with an exploration of the very concept that underlies these financial instruments.

Section 1: Definition and Basics of REITs

Understanding the Concept of Real Estate Investment Trusts (REITs)

1.1.1 Definition and Core Characteristics

At its core, a Real Estate Investment Trust (REIT) is a company that owns, operates, or finances income-generating real estate. The concept of REITs was introduced in the United States in 1960 as a way to provide individuals with the opportunity to invest in large-scale, income-producing real estate without having to buy, manage, or finance properties directly. One of the defining characteristics of REITs is their special tax treatment, allowing them to avoid corporate income taxes if they distribute at least 90% of their taxable income to shareholders in the form of dividends.

REITs can take various forms, including equity REITs, mortgage REITs, and hybrid REITs. Equity REITs primarily own and manage income-producing real estate, while mortgage REITs invest in real estate-related debt. Hybrid REITs combine elements of both equity and mortgage REITs, offering a diversified approach to real estate investing.

1.1.2 Legal Structure and Requirements

To qualify as a REIT, a company must adhere to specific legal requirements outlined in the Internal Revenue Code. These requirements include:

- **Asset Composition**: At least 75% of a REIT's total assets must be invested in real estate, cash, or U.S. Treasuries.
- **Income Distribution**: The REIT must distribute at least 90% of its taxable income annually in the form of dividends to shareholders.
- **Shareholder Requirements**: A REIT must have at least 100 shareholders, and no more than 50% of its shares can be held by five or fewer individuals.
- **Management Structure**: REITs must be managed by a board of directors or trustees.

These legal requirements ensure that REITs operate in a manner consistent with their purpose of providing widespread access to real estate investments.

1.1.3 Key Components of a REIT

Understanding the key components of a REIT is essential for investors looking to navigate this specialized sector of the financial markets.

- **Assets**: The primary assets of a REIT are income-generating real estate properties. These can include residential and commercial properties, shopping centers, office buildings, hotels, and more.

- **Dividends**: Unlike traditional stocks, where investors benefit from capital appreciation, the primary source of return for REIT investors is in the form of dividends. These dividends are generated from the rental income and capital gains realized by the underlying real estate properties.
- **Shares**: REITs are traded on major stock exchanges, and investors can buy shares in the open market, providing them with a liquid and easily accessible form of real estate investment.
- **Management Team**: REITs are managed by boards of directors or trustees responsible for overseeing the company's operations, property acquisitions, and overall strategy.

In essence, REITs serve as a vehicle for individuals to pool their resources and collectively invest in a diversified portfolio of income-producing real estate, offering the benefits of real estate ownership without the need for significant capital or direct involvement in property management.

Section 2: Overview of Real Estate Investment Trusts (REITs)

In the world of finance, Real Estate Investment Trusts (REITs) stand out as unique investment vehicles that provide individuals with a means to access the real estate market without the complexities of direct property ownership. As we delve into this section, we aim to break down the structure of REITs, offering a comprehensive understanding of the various types, core operations, and distinctive features that characterize these investment entities.

Breaking Down the Structure of REITs

Real Estate Investment Trusts are structured entities that play a pivotal role in channeling investment into the real estate sector. Understanding the intricacies of their structure is crucial for investors seeking exposure to the diverse opportunities that the real estate market presents.

1.2.1 Identifying Different Types of REITs

REITs come in various forms, each catering to specific niches within the real estate market. Identifying these types is essential for investors looking to tailor their portfolios to specific investment objectives.

- **Equity REITs**: These are the most common types of REITs. Equity REITs primarily own and operate income-generating real estate properties. These can include residential properties, commercial office spaces, shopping centers, and other real estate assets. The revenue generated comes from renting out these properties, and investors in equity REITs benefit from dividends based on rental income and potential capital appreciation.
- **Mortgage REITs**: Unlike equity REITs, mortgage REITs invest in real estate-related debt, such as mortgages and mortgage-backed securities. Their income is derived from the interest earned on these investments. Mortgage REITs *do not own physical properties* but instead provide financing for real estate transactions. This type of REIT is more sensitive to interest rate fluctuations and economic conditions.
- **Hybrid REITs**: As the name suggests, hybrid REITs combine elements of both equity and mortgage REITs. This provides investors with a diversified approach, allowing them to benefit from both rental income and interest from real estate-related

debt.

Understanding the distinctions between these types allows investors to align their portfolios with their specific risk tolerance, investment goals, and market expectations.

1.2.2 Core Operations and Business Model

The core operations of a REIT revolve around acquiring, managing, and, in the case of equity REITs, owning income-generating real estate. This operational structure is crucial to the success of a REIT and shapes its business model.

- **Property Acquisition**: REITs continually seek opportunities to acquire real estate assets that align with their investment strategy. This involves thorough market research, due diligence, and financial analysis to ensure that the potential acquisition complements the overall portfolio.
- **Property Management**: For those REITs that own physical properties, effective management is paramount. This includes tasks such as tenant management, property maintenance, and ensuring compliance with regulatory requirements. Well-managed properties contribute to a steady stream of rental income.
- **Dividend Distribution**: One of the distinguishing features of REITs is their obligation to distribute at least 90% of their taxable income to shareholders in the form of dividends. This distribution provides investors with a consistent income stream, making REITs an attractive option for those seeking passive income.

1.2.3 Unique Features of REIT Investments

Investing in REITs offers unique features that set them apart from other asset classes. These features contribute to the appeal of REITs among a diverse range of investors.

- **Liquidity**: REITs are traded on major stock exchanges, providing investors with liquidity that is not typically associated with direct real estate ownership. This allows investors to buy and sell REIT shares easily, making them a more flexible investment option.
- **Diversification**: By investing in a REIT, individuals gain exposure to a diversified portfolio of real estate assets. This diversification can mitigate risks associated with concentrated investments in specific properties or sectors.
- **Accessibility**: Unlike purchasing physical real estate, investing in REITs requires a lower capital outlay. This accessibility makes REITs an attractive option for individuals who may not have the financial means to buy entire properties but still want to participate in real estate markets.
- **Tax Advantages**: The unique tax structure of REITs allows them to avoid corporate income taxes if they distribute at least 90% of their taxable income to shareholders. This tax efficiency enhances the overall returns for investors.

The foundation laid in understanding the structure and operations of REITs will serve as a valuable guide for investors navigating the complexities of real estate investments.

Section 3: Benefits of Investing in REITs for Beginners

Embarking on the journey of investing in Real Estate Investment Trusts (REITs) opens up a world of opportunities for beginners seeking exposure to the real estate market. In this section, we delve into the myriad benefits that make REITs an attractive and accessible option for those new to the realm of investing.

Exploring the Advantages of REIT Investments

Real Estate Investment Trusts have gained prominence for good reason, offering a range of advantages that align with the financial goals and preferences of novice investors. Let's explore these advantages in detail.

1.3.1 Diversification Opportunities

One of the key benefits that REITs bring to the table is the opportunity for diversification. Diversifying a portfolio involves spreading investments across different asset classes to reduce risk. REITs, by their very nature, provide exposure to a diverse range of real estate assets.

- *Asset Class Diversification*: REITs cover various sectors within the real estate market, including residential, commercial, retail, healthcare, and infrastructure. This diversity helps investors avoid concentration risk in a single type of property.
- *Geographical Diversification*: REITs may own properties in different geographic regions, providing investors with exposure to varied real estate markets. This geographic diversification helps mitigate risks associated with localized economic downturns or real estate market fluctuations.

For beginners, the ability to achieve diversification through a single investment vehicle like a REIT is particularly advantageous. It allows them to spread their investment across a broad spectrum of real estate assets without the need for substantial capital or the complexities of managing multiple properties.

1.3.2 Accessibility for Small Investors

One of the most democratizing aspects of REIT investing is its accessibility, making real estate a viable option for investors with limited capital.

- *Lower Capital Requirements*: Unlike direct property ownership, which often demands significant upfront capital for property acquisition, REITs allow individuals to invest in real estate with a relatively modest amount. This accessibility lowers the barrier to entry for small investors who might otherwise be excluded from the real estate market.
- *Fractional Ownership*: REITs enable investors to own a fraction of multiple properties within the portfolio. This fractional ownership model allows beginners to participate in a diversified real estate portfolio without the need to buy entire properties.
- *Ease of Entry and Exit*: Investing in REITs is as simple as buying and selling stocks on the stock market. This ease of entry and exit provides small investors with the flexibility to adjust their investment portfolio based on changing financial goals or market conditions.

For beginners looking to dip their toes into real estate without committing substantial capital, REITs offer a pathway to participate in the potential returns of the real estate market.

1.3.3 Passive Income Potential

Passive income is a central allure of REIT investing, providing investors with a consistent stream of income generated from rental payments and other real estate-related activities.

- *Steady Dividend Income*: REITs are required to distribute at least 90% of their taxable income to shareholders in the form of dividends. This income distribution mechanism results in regular and often higher-than-average dividend yields compared to many other stocks.
- *Predictable Cash Flow*: Real estate, as an asset class, often generates predictable and steady cash flows. This stability is reflected in the dividends paid by REITs, making them an attractive option for investors seeking reliable income.
- *Diversified Income Sources*: The diverse nature of REIT portfolios, spanning various property types and sectors, contributes to diversified income sources. This diversification can enhance the stability of passive income streams.

For beginners, the appeal of passive income aligns with the desire for financial stability and ongoing returns. REITs provide a pathway for individuals to build a source of passive income over time, making them an attractive option for those looking to supplement their earnings or plan for retirement.

1.3.4 Liquidity and Marketability

Liquidity is a crucial factor for investors, especially beginners, who may need to access their funds or make changes to their investment portfolio.

- *Publicly Traded Securities*: REITs are publicly traded on major stock exchanges, providing investors with the ability to buy and sell shares with ease. This liquidity allows investors to convert their holdings into cash quickly, providing flexibility in responding to changing financial needs.
- *Marketability and Transparency*: As publicly traded securities, REITs are subject to market forces, ensuring transparency in their valuation. This market-driven valuation provides investors with real-time information about the value of their investments.
- *No Lock-In Periods*: Unlike certain real estate investment structures that may involve lock-in periods, REIT investors can enter or exit their positions at any time during market hours. This flexibility aligns with the dynamic nature of financial markets.

For beginners, the liquidity and marketability of REITs offer peace of mind, knowing that their investments are not tied up in illiquid assets. This feature also facilitates the ability to make strategic adjustments to the investment portfolio based on changing market conditions.

In conclusion, the benefits of investing in REITs for beginners are multifaceted. From providing diversification and accessibility to offering passive income potential and liquidity, REITs offer a compelling entry point for individuals looking to venture into real estate investments.

Section 4: Brief History and Evolution of REITs

Real Estate Investment Trusts (REITs) have a rich history that traces their roots back several decades. Understanding the historical context and evolution of REITs provides valuable insights into the factors that have shaped their development into the prominent investment vehicles we recognize today.

Tracing the Roots and Development of REITs

1.4.1 Historical Context and Origins

The concept of Real Estate Investment Trusts originated in the United States in the early 1960s as a result of the intersection of economic needs and legislative innovation.

- **Pre-REIT Era**: Before the creation of REITs, investing in large-scale real estate projects was largely restricted to institutional investors and wealthy individuals. The real estate market lacked a mechanism that would allow a broader spectrum of investors to access and benefit from income-generating real estate.
- **Land Utilization Act of 1960**: The catalyst for the creation of REITs was the Land Utilization Act of 1960, which introduced the framework for these investment vehicles. The primary motivation behind this legislative initiative was to provide individual investors with an opportunity to participate in the economic benefits of large-scale, professionally managed real estate projects.

1.4.2 Milestones in the Evolution of REITs

The evolution of REITs can be marked by key milestones that reflect their growing significance in the financial landscape.

- **First REITs Formed (1960s-1970s)**: The first REITs were established in the early 1960s, and by the end of that decade, several more had been formed. Initially, REITs focused on traditional property types such as residential and commercial real estate.

- **Tax Reform Act of 1986**: A pivotal moment in the history of REITs came with the Tax Reform Act of 1986. This legislation clarified and solidified the tax benefits of REITs, stipulating that they must distribute at least 95% of their taxable income to shareholders. The Act also expanded the types of properties that could qualify for REIT status.
- **Global Expansion (1990s-2000s)**: The success of the REIT model in the United States led to its adoption in other countries. The 1990s and 2000s witnessed the global expansion of the REIT structure, with various countries implementing their versions of REIT legislation.
- **REIT Modernization Act (1999)**: In response to changing market dynamics, the REIT Modernization Act was enacted in 1999. This legislation increased flexibility for REITs, allowing them to engage in a broader range of activities and investments.
- **Global Financial Crisis (2008-2009)**: The global financial crisis had a significant impact on the real estate market and, by extension, on REITs. The crisis underscored the sensitivity of REITs to economic conditions and prompted adjustments in their strategies.
- **Continued Growth and Innovation (2010s-2020s)**: In recent years, REITs have continued to evolve, embracing technological advancements, and diversifying into new and non-traditional real estate sectors. This ongoing evolution reflects the adaptability of REITs to changing market dynamics.

1.4.3 Influential Factors Shaping the REIT Landscape

Several factors have played a crucial role in shaping the landscape of REITs, contributing to their growth, resilience, and adaptability.

- **Democratization of Real Estate**: REITs have been instrumental in democratizing access to real estate investments. By allowing small investors to participate in income-generating real estate without the burden of direct ownership, REITs have broadened the investor base.
- **Tax Advantages**: The tax advantages afforded to REITs, particularly the avoidance of corporate income taxes through the distribution of dividends, have been a fundamental factor in their attractiveness. This tax-efficient structure enhances returns for investors.
- **Market Dynamics and Economic Conditions**: The performance of REITs is closely tied to broader economic conditions and market dynamics. Factors such as interest rates, economic growth, and real estate trends influence the profitability and strategic decisions of REITs.
- **Technological Advancements**: The integration of technology, commonly referred to as PropTech, has played a transformative role in the real estate sector. REITs have embraced technological innovations in property management, data analysis, and market research to enhance operational efficiency and decision-making.
- **Globalization of Real Estate Markets**: The globalization of real estate markets has influenced the expansion of REITs beyond national borders. Investors now have opportunities to diversify their portfolios with international REIT investments, providing exposure to different geographic regions and market conditions.
- **Changing Consumer Behavior and Industry Trends**: Shifts

in consumer behavior, such as the rise of e-commerce and remote work trends, have influenced the types of real estate properties that are in demand. REITs, adapting to these trends, have diversified their portfolios to include properties aligned with evolving consumer preferences.

Understanding the historical trajectory and influential factors behind the development of REITs provides a comprehensive perspective for investors.

Chapter 2: Types of REITs

Section 1: Residential REITs

Investing in real estate offers a diverse range of opportunities, and Residential Real Estate Investment Trusts (REITs) stand out as a distinct category within this landscape. In this section, we explore Residential REITs, unraveling their focus on apartment buildings and multi-family properties, the dynamics of rental income, and the factors that influence their performance.

Understanding Residential Real Estate Investment Trusts

2.1.1 Focus on Apartment Buildings and Multi-Family Properties

Residential REITs, as the name suggests, concentrate on residential properties, specifically apartment buildings and multi-family housing complexes. These REITs invest in, own, and manage a portfolio of residential real estate assets with the primary objective of generating rental income. The multi-family nature of these properties provides a unique investment proposition.

- *Apartment Buildings*: Residential REITs often include apartment buildings in their portfolios. These can range from small complexes to large, high-rise structures. The appeal of apartment buildings lies in their potential for consistent rental income and the ability to accommodate a diverse tenant base.
- *Multi-Family Properties*: Beyond standalone apartment buildings, Residential REITs may invest in smaller multi-family housing developments. These can include townhouses,

condominiums, or other structures that house multiple families within a single property.

The focus on residential assets distinguishes these REITs from others that may concentrate on commercial real estate, such as office buildings, retail spaces, or industrial properties.

2.1.2 Rental Income and Tenant Dynamics

The core revenue stream for Residential REITs comes from the rental income generated by leasing residential units to tenants. Understanding the dynamics of this rental income is crucial for evaluating the performance and potential profitability of Residential REITs.

- *Stability of Rental Income*: Residential properties, especially multi-family units, often provide a stable and predictable source of rental income. The demand for housing, driven by population growth, migration patterns, and lifestyle preferences, contributes to the stability of rental income.
- *Tenant Diversity*: Residential REITs benefit from tenant diversity within their properties. With multiple units catering to various household sizes and demographics, these REITs can adapt to changes in demand and preferences among renters.
- *Lease Agreements*: Lease agreements with tenants outline the terms of occupancy, rental rates, and other conditions. The contractual nature of these agreements provides a level of predictability for Residential REITs, allowing them to plan for future cash flows.

Understanding tenant dynamics is crucial for Residential REITs to tailor their offerings to the needs of the rental market. Factors such as location, amenities, and rental pricing strategies play a significant role in attracting and retaining tenants.

2.1.3 Factors Influencing Residential REIT Performance

Several factors influence the performance of Residential REITs, reflecting the interconnected nature of real estate markets and broader economic trends.

- *Local Real Estate Market Conditions*: The performance of Residential REITs is intricately tied to the conditions of the local real estate market. Factors such as population growth, employment opportunities, and housing demand within specific regions significantly impact the occupancy rates and rental income of residential properties.
- *Interest Rates and Financing Costs*: Residential REITs are affected by changes in interest rates, as these rates influence the cost of financing for property acquisitions. In a low-interest-rate environment, REITs may find favorable financing terms, contributing to their profitability.
- *Macro-Economic Trends*: Economic trends, including GDP growth, inflation, and consumer spending, can influence the performance of Residential REITs. Economic downturns may lead to changes in housing demand and affordability, affecting occupancy rates and rental income.
- *Technological and Lifestyle Trends*: Evolving technological trends and shifts in lifestyle preferences also play a role in Residential REIT performance. Amenities such as smart home features, co-working spaces, and proximity to urban centers may become increasingly important considerations for renters.

As investors evaluate Residential REITs, a comprehensive analysis of these factors is essential to gauge the potential risks and rewards associated with this specific sector of the real estate market. The stability of rental income, coupled with the adaptability of Residential REITs to changing market dynamics, makes them a compelling option for those seeking exposure to the residential real estate asset class.

Section 2: Commercial REITs

Commercial Real Estate Investment Trusts (REITs) form a crucial segment within the real estate investment landscape, focusing on income-generating properties tailored for commercial use. In this section, we delve into Commercial REITs, exploring their investments in office buildings, retail spaces, industrial properties, and the intricate dynamics of lease structures and tenant relationships.

Delving into Commercial Real Estate Investment Trusts

2.2.1 Office Buildings and Corporate Spaces

Commercial REITs, with their emphasis on commercial properties, often include office buildings and corporate spaces within their portfolios. These properties cater to businesses seeking strategically located and professionally managed spaces to conduct their operations.

- *Office Buildings*: Commercial REITs invest in a range of office buildings, from downtown high-rises to suburban office parks. The appeal of office buildings lies in their potential for stable, long-term leases with corporate tenants. The location, amenities, and quality of these office spaces contribute to their desirability among businesses.
- *Corporate Spaces*: Beyond traditional office buildings,

Commercial REITs may own and manage corporate campuses or specialized corporate spaces. These properties are often designed to meet the unique needs of specific industries or large corporate tenants.

The success of Commercial REITs with office properties is closely tied to the demand for office space, influenced by economic trends, corporate expansion, and shifts in workplace preferences.

2.2.2 Retail Spaces and Shopping Centers

Commercial REITs also play a significant role in the retail sector, investing in properties such as shopping centers, malls, and standalone retail spaces. The retail focus brings its own set of considerations and opportunities.

- *Shopping Centers and Malls*: Commercial REITs often own and manage shopping centers and malls, attracting a diverse array of retailers. The success of these properties is tied to factors such as consumer foot traffic, retail trends, and the mix of tenants. Well-positioned shopping centers with a mix of anchor tenants and specialty retailers can thrive in dynamic retail environments.
- *Standalone Retail Spaces*: In addition to larger shopping centers, Commercial REITs may invest in standalone retail spaces. These can range from single-tenant buildings to smaller strip malls. The dynamics of standalone retail properties are influenced by local demographics, consumer behavior, and the overall health of the retail industry.

Investing in retail spaces requires a keen understanding of consumer trends, online competition, and the ability to adapt to the evolving retail landscape.

2.2.3 Industrial and Warehouse Properties

The rise of e-commerce and changes in supply chain dynamics have elevated the importance of industrial and warehouse properties. Commercial REITs strategically invest in these types of properties to capitalize on the growing demand for logistics and distribution spaces.

- *Industrial Properties*: Commercial REITs may own and manage industrial properties, which include manufacturing facilities, warehouses, and distribution centers. These properties serve as critical components of the supply chain, providing storage and distribution solutions for goods.
- *Warehouse Spaces*: With the growth of e-commerce, the demand for warehouse spaces has surged. Commercial REITs involved in the industrial sector often focus on acquiring and developing warehouse spaces strategically located to facilitate efficient distribution for companies such as Amazon.

The success of Commercial REITs in the industrial sector hinges on the integration of technology, transportation infrastructure, and the ability to meet the evolving needs of e-commerce and global trade.

2.2.4 Analyzing Lease Structures and Tenant Relationships

The financial performance of Commercial REITs is intricately tied to the lease structures they establish with tenants. Analyzing these lease agreements and fostering strong tenant relationships are crucial aspects of managing commercial properties.

- *Lease Structures*: Commercial leases can take various forms, influencing the revenue stability and growth potential for Commercial REITs. Common lease structures include:
    - **Triple Net Leases (NNN)**: Tenants bear the responsibility for property taxes, insurance, and maintenance costs in addition to rent.
    - **Gross Leases**: The landlord covers property expenses, and the tenant pays a fixed rent.
    - **Percentage Leases**: Rent is calculated as a percentage of the tenant's sales.
- *Tenant Relationships*: Building and maintaining positive relationships with tenants are vital for Commercial REITs. Tenant satisfaction, lease renewals, and attracting high-quality tenants contribute to the overall success of the REIT. Strong tenant relationships can lead to long-term occupancy, reducing vacancy risks and enhancing the stability of rental income.

Understanding the nuances of lease structures and fostering positive tenant relationships require proactive property management and strategic decision-making. Commercial REITs often engage in comprehensive market research to identify tenant needs and trends, enabling them to position their properties competitively.

In conclusion, Commercial REITs offer investors exposure to a diverse range of income-generating properties tailored for commercial use. The success of these REITs is closely tied to economic trends, corporate activities, and the ability to adapt to changes in consumer behavior and retail dynamics.

Section 3: Retail REITs

Retail Real Estate Investment Trusts (REITs) form a distinct category within the broader real estate investment landscape, focusing on properties designed for retail and consumer-oriented businesses. In this section, we navigate the world of Retail REITs, exploring their investments in malls and shopping complexes, the significance of tenant mix and consumer trends, the impact of e-commerce on Retail REITs, and the key metrics for assessing their performance.

Navigating the World of Retail Real Estate Investment Trusts

2.3.1 Investing in Malls and Shopping Complexes

Retail REITs specialize in properties that cater to retail and consumer-driven businesses. These can include malls, shopping centers, and standalone retail spaces. Understanding the dynamics of investing in these properties provides valuable insights into the functioning of Retail REITs.

- *Malls and Shopping Complexes*: One of the primary focuses of Retail REITs is investing in and managing malls and shopping complexes. These properties typically house a variety of retailers, ranging from department stores and specialty shops to dining establishments. The success of these spaces depends on factors such as location, foot traffic, and the overall consumer experience.
- *Standalone Retail Spaces*: In addition to larger shopping complexes, Retail REITs may also invest in standalone retail spaces. These can range from single-tenant buildings to smaller strip malls. The dynamics of standalone retail

properties are influenced by factors such as location, tenant mix, and local consumer demographics.

The performance of Retail REITs is closely tied to the vibrancy and attractiveness of the retail spaces they own and manage.

2.3.2 Tenant Mix and Consumer Trends

The composition of tenants within retail properties, often referred to as the tenant mix, plays a pivotal role in the success of Retail REITs. Additionally, understanding consumer trends is essential for shaping the tenant mix and adapting to changing market dynamics.

- *Tenant Mix Strategy*: Retail REITs strategically curate the tenant mix within their properties to create a balanced and appealing shopping environment. This involves attracting anchor tenants, which are large, well-known retailers, as well as a diverse array of specialty stores. The goal is to offer consumers a comprehensive and satisfying shopping experience.
- *Adapting to Consumer Trends*: Retail REITs must stay attuned to evolving consumer trends. Changes in shopping behavior, preferences for online or in-person experiences, and shifts in the types of products and services consumers seek can impact the success of retail properties. Adapting to these trends requires flexibility in adjusting the tenant mix and amenities offered within retail spaces.

Understanding the interplay between tenant mix and consumer trends enables Retail REITs to position their properties as appealing destinations for shoppers, fostering sustained foot traffic and tenant success.

2.3.3 E-commerce Impact on Retail REITs

The rise of e-commerce has reshaped the retail landscape, posing both challenges and opportunities for Retail REITs. Navigating this impact requires strategic planning and adaptability.

- *Challenges Posed by E-commerce*: The convenience of online shopping has led to challenges for traditional brick-and-mortar retailers. Some tenants within retail properties may face competition from e-commerce platforms, affecting their ability to attract customers to physical stores.
- *Opportunities in Last-Mile Distribution*: On the flip side, the growth of e-commerce has created opportunities for Retail REITs in the realm of last-mile distribution. Properties strategically located for efficient order fulfillment and delivery hubs become valuable assets in the e-commerce supply chain.
- *Adaptation Strategies*: Retail REITs have adapted to the e-commerce impact by incorporating technology, enhancing the online presence of tenants, and exploring partnerships with e-commerce platforms. Additionally, creating experiential retail spaces and offering unique in-person experiences have become strategies to attract consumers who value the tactile and social aspects of shopping.

Effectively managing the impact of e-commerce requires Retail REITs to be proactive in their approach, fostering collaboration with tenants and staying abreast of technological advancements in the retail sector.

2.3.4 Assessing Retail REIT Performance Metrics

Evaluating the performance of Retail REITs involves analyzing key metrics that provide insights into the financial health and operational efficiency of these investment vehicles.

- *Occupancy Rates*: The occupancy rate reflects the percentage of leased space within retail properties. High occupancy rates indicate strong tenant demand and a vibrant retail environment.
- *Same-Store Sales Growth*: This metric measures the revenue growth of tenants within the same retail properties over a specific period. Positive same-store sales growth is an indicator of the overall health and performance of the retail space.
- *Lease Expirations and Renewals*: Understanding the timing of lease expirations and the rate of lease renewals provides insights into the stability of rental income for Retail REITs. High lease renewal rates contribute to income predictability.
- *Foot Traffic and Sales per Square Foot*: These metrics gauge the vibrancy of retail properties. High foot traffic and strong sales per square foot indicate that the retail space is attracting consumers and generating revenue.
- *Debt and Financing Ratios*: Assessing the level of debt and financing structures helps evaluate the financial leverage of Retail REITs. Prudent debt management is crucial for long-term sustainability.

By monitoring these performance metrics, investors can gain a comprehensive understanding of how Retail REITs are navigating market dynamics, responding to consumer trends, and managing the complexities of the retail sector.

In conclusion, Retail REITs offer investors exposure to the dynamic world of retail properties. The success of these REITs hinges on effective tenant management, adaptation to consumer trends, and strategic responses to the impact of e-commerce.

Section 4: Healthcare REITs

Healthcare Real Estate Investment Trusts (REITs) constitute a distinctive sector within the real estate investment landscape, focusing on properties that cater to the healthcare industry. In this section, we explore Healthcare REITs, delving into their investments in hospitals and medical facilities, senior housing, and assisted living properties. Additionally, we examine the influence of demographic trends on the opportunities presented by Healthcare REITs.

Exploring Healthcare Real Estate Investment Trusts

2.4.1 Investment in Hospitals and Medical Facilities

Healthcare REITs distinguish themselves by investing in properties that support the delivery of medical services. These can include hospitals, medical office buildings, and other facilities critical to the healthcare infrastructure.

- *Hospitals*: Healthcare REITs may own and manage hospitals, which are essential components of the healthcare system. Hospitals represent significant real estate assets, and their strategic location, capacity, and specialized services contribute to their appeal for Healthcare REIT investments.
- *Medical Office Buildings*: Healthcare services often extend beyond hospitals to medical office buildings (MOBs). These properties house a variety of medical practices, clinics, and

outpatient services. Healthcare REITs involved in medical office investments benefit from the demand for accessible healthcare services in local communities.

The investment in hospitals and medical facilities aligns with the broader goal of Healthcare REITs to contribute to the improvement and accessibility of healthcare services.

2.4.2 Senior Housing and Assisted Living Properties

With an aging population, the demand for senior housing and assisted living facilities has grown, and Healthcare REITs play a pivotal role in meeting this demand.

- *Senior Housing*: Healthcare REITs invest in senior housing properties designed to accommodate the unique needs of older adults. These may include independent living communities, where residents maintain a degree of autonomy, as well as more comprehensive senior housing options that provide additional assistance and healthcare services.
- *Assisted Living Properties*: Assisted living properties offer a higher level of support and care for seniors who need assistance with daily activities. Healthcare REITs involved in assisted living investments contribute to the provision of a supportive and safe environment for seniors.

Investing in senior housing and assisted living properties reflects the commitment of Healthcare REITs to address the evolving healthcare needs of an aging population.

2.4.3 Demographic Trends and Healthcare REIT Opportunities

Demographic trends, particularly the aging of the population, significantly influence the opportunities and growth potential for Healthcare REITs.

- *Aging Population*: The aging of the baby boomer generation has led to an increased demand for healthcare services and facilities catering to older adults. Healthcare REITs strategically position themselves to capitalize on this demographic trend by investing in properties that align with the healthcare needs of seniors.
- *Increased Healthcare Spending*: As individuals age, there is typically an increase in healthcare spending. Healthcare REITs benefit from this trend as the demand for medical facilities, senior housing, and assisted living properties rises.
- *Focus on Wellness and Preventive Care*: Beyond traditional healthcare facilities, there is a growing emphasis on wellness and preventive care. Healthcare REITs may explore investments in properties that support these evolving trends, such as medical wellness centers and facilities offering holistic healthcare services.
- *Adaptability to Changing Healthcare Models*: The healthcare industry is undergoing transformations, including shifts towards outpatient care, telemedicine, and community-based healthcare models. Healthcare REITs with the flexibility to adapt to these changing models can identify new opportunities for investments.

By staying attuned to demographic trends and the evolving landscape of healthcare delivery, Healthcare REITs position themselves as key players in addressing the diverse healthcare needs of communities.

In conclusion, Healthcare REITs play a crucial role in supporting the healthcare infrastructure by investing in properties that contribute to the well-being of individuals across different life stages. Whether through hospitals, medical office buildings, senior housing, or assisted living properties, Healthcare REITs align their investments with the demographic trends and healthcare demands of the population.

Section 5: Infrastructure REITs

Infrastructure Real Estate Investment Trusts (REITs) form a specialized category within the real estate investment landscape, focusing on essential infrastructure assets critical to the functioning of societies. In this section, we delve into Infrastructure REITs, investigating their focus on essential infrastructure assets, their involvement in energy, utilities, and communication infrastructure, and the long-term stability and income potential they offer.

Investigating Infrastructure Real Estate Investment Trusts

2.5.1 Focus on Essential Infrastructure Assets

Infrastructure REITs concentrate on investing in and managing essential infrastructure assets that provide fundamental services and support the daily operations of communities and industries.

- *Transportation Infrastructure*: This category includes investments in toll roads, bridges, tunnels, and other transportation-related assets. Infrastructure REITs contribute to the development and maintenance of transportation networks that facilitate the movement of people and goods.
- *Utilities Infrastructure*: Infrastructure REITs may invest in utilities such as water and wastewater facilities, providing crucial services for residential, commercial, and industrial

properties. These investments contribute to the reliable delivery of essential resources.

- *Social Infrastructure*: Social infrastructure investments may encompass properties such as schools, hospitals, and government buildings. While these assets serve public needs, they also offer stable, long-term income potential for Infrastructure REITs.

The focus on essential infrastructure assets distinguishes Infrastructure REITs from other types, emphasizing their role in supporting the fundamental needs of societies.

2.5.2 Energy, Utilities, and Communication Infrastructure

Infrastructure REITs play a significant role in energy, utilities, and communication infrastructure, contributing to the development and maintenance of facilities that power economies and connect communities.

- *Energy Infrastructure*: This includes investments in energy-related assets such as power plants, pipelines, and renewable energy facilities. Infrastructure REITs involved in energy infrastructure contribute to the generation, transmission, and distribution of energy resources.
- *Utilities Infrastructure*: Beyond water facilities, utilities infrastructure for Infrastructure REITs may extend to electric and gas utilities. Investing in these assets aligns with the goal of providing reliable and essential services to communities.
- *Communication Infrastructure*: Infrastructure REITs may invest in communication-related assets, such as cell towers, data centers, and fiber optic networks. As the demand for connectivity and digital services grows, these investments

become integral to supporting modern communication needs.

Participating in these critical infrastructure sectors not only aligns with societal needs but also positions Infrastructure REITs as key contributors to the sustainability and efficiency of essential services.

2.5.3 Long-Term Stability and Income Potential

One of the distinguishing features of Infrastructure REITs is their emphasis on long-term stability and income potential. The nature of essential infrastructure assets contributes to the resilience and predictability of these investments.

- *Stable and Predictable Cash Flows*: Infrastructure REITs often benefit from stable and predictable cash flows generated by essential services. Toll roads, utilities, and communication infrastructure, for example, generate revenue through long-term contracts, providing a consistent income stream for investors.
- *Inflation Hedge*: Infrastructure assets, particularly those linked to utilities and essential services, can serve as a hedge against inflation. The long-term nature of these investments, combined with potential for periodic rate adjustments, allows Infrastructure REITs to align with economic changes.
- *Long-Term Capital Appreciation*: Beyond income potential, Infrastructure REITs may experience long-term capital appreciation as the value of essential infrastructure assets tends to appreciate over time. Population growth, urbanization, and increased demand for services contribute to the appreciation of these assets.

The long-term stability and income potential of Infrastructure REITs make them attractive options for investors seeking a balance between capital preservation and income generation.

In conclusion, Infrastructure REITs occupy a unique position within the real estate investment landscape, focusing on assets that form the backbone of societies. Their investments in essential infrastructure assets, spanning transportation, utilities, energy, and communication, contribute to the stability and functionality of communities.

Section 6: Specialized and Hybrid REITs

Real Estate Investment Trusts (REITs) have evolved beyond traditional residential and commercial sectors, giving rise to specialized and hybrid REITs. In this section, we delve into the unique realm of these investment vehicles, exploring Special Purpose REITs, Hybrid REITs, and the nuanced considerations associated with their risk and return profiles.

2.6.1 Special Purpose REITs (Data Centers, Timber, etc.)

Special Purpose REITs focus on niche sectors, catering to specific industries or asset classes. Data Centers REITs, for instance, capitalize on the growing demand for digital infrastructure. These REITs own and manage facilities that house servers and data storage equipment, critical components of the digital age. As the reliance on data continues to surge, investing in Data Centers REITs provides exposure to a sector with substantial growth potential.

Timber REITs represent another facet of specialization. By owning and managing timberland, these REITs benefit from the timber industry's cyclical nature. They generate income through timber sales and, in some cases, through recreational leases. Timber REITs often offer investors a unique combination of capital appreciation and sustainable income, making them an attractive component for diversified portfolios.

2.6.2 Hybrid REITs Combining Multiple Property Types

Hybrid REITs represent a fusion of different property types within a single investment vehicle. Rather than limiting themselves to a specific sector, these REITs diversify across various real estate categories. For example, a Hybrid REIT might combine residential, commercial, and healthcare properties within its portfolio.

This diversification strategy aims to mitigate risk by spreading investments across different real estate sectors, each responding differently to market fluctuations. By combining the income stability of commercial properties with the growth potential of residential and the resilience of healthcare, Hybrid REITs seek to create a well-balanced and resilient investment option.

2.6.3 Assessing Risk and Return Profiles of Specialized REITs

While specialized REITs offer unique investment opportunities, they also come with specific risk considerations. Understanding and assessing these risks is crucial for investors looking to navigate the specialized and hybrid landscape effectively.

2.6.3.1 Industry-Specific Risks

Specialized REITs often face risks tied to their specific industry. For instance, Data Centers REITs may be vulnerable to technological advancements that reduce the need for physical data storage. Timber REITs might be influenced by factors like climate change, affecting timber growth cycles. Investors in specialized REITs should conduct thorough research on the industry dynamics to gauge potential risks accurately.

2.6.3.2 Regulatory and Environmental Risks

Certain specialized sectors, such as healthcare or energy infrastructure, may be subject to specific regulations. Investors need to stay attuned to regulatory changes that could impact the performance of specialized REITs. Additionally, environmental considerations, such as the sustainability of timber practices or the ecological impact of data centers, play a role in assessing long-term viability.

2.6.3.3 Market Conditions and Economic Trends

The performance of specialized REITs can be influenced by broader market conditions and economic trends. Changes in consumer behavior, technological advancements, or economic downturns may affect specific sectors differently. Investors must evaluate how external factors might impact the specialized niche in which a REIT operates.

2.6.3.4 Liquidity and Trade Considerations

Some specialized REITs may exhibit lower liquidity compared to their more mainstream counterparts. Investors should consider the ease of buying or selling shares, especially during volatile market conditions. Additionally, understanding the trading dynamics of specialized REITs is crucial for effective portfolio management.

In conclusion, Specialized and Hybrid REITs offer investors the opportunity to tailor their portfolios to specific industries or achieve diversification through a blend of property types. However, these investments come with their own set of challenges, including industry-specific risks, regulatory considerations, market sensitivity, and liquidity concerns. As with any investment, due diligence and a comprehensive understanding of the underlying assets are essential for making informed decisions in the specialized and hybrid REIT space. By carefully assessing the risk and return profiles, investors can strategically incorporate these specialized instruments into their portfolios, harnessing the unique advantages they bring to the broader realm of real estate investing.

Section 7: Choosing the Right Type for Your Investment Goals

Investing in Real Estate Investment Trusts (REITs) offers a diverse array of opportunities, each catering to specific investment goals and risk tolerances. In this section, we delve into the process of choosing the right type of REIT to align with individual investment objectives. This includes aligning REIT investments with financial goals, balancing risk and return, and employing strategies for diversification within REIT types.

Tailoring Your Portfolio to Meet Investment Objectives

2.7.1 Aligning REIT Investments with Financial Goals

One of the first considerations in choosing the right type of REIT is aligning the investments with your financial goals. Different types of REITs offer distinct risk and return profiles, catering to a range of investment objectives.

- *Income Generation*: If your primary goal is to generate a consistent stream of passive income, consider REITs that focus on income-producing properties, such as residential,

commercial, or healthcare REITs. These sectors often offer stable rental income, making them suitable for investors seeking regular dividends.
- *Capital Appreciation*: For investors focused on long-term capital appreciation, sectors like infrastructure or specialized REITs may be appealing. These investments often exhibit stability and have the potential for appreciation over time, driven by factors such as population growth and increasing demand for specific assets.
- *Balanced Growth and Income*: Hybrid REITs, combining multiple property types, can provide a balanced approach for investors seeking both growth and income. These REITs diversify across sectors, offering exposure to different market dynamics.

Understanding your financial goals allows you to narrow down the types of REITs that best fit your investment strategy.

2.7.2 Balancing Risk and Return

Choosing the right type of REIT involves a careful consideration of risk and return dynamics. Different sectors within the REIT universe carry varying levels of risk, and investors should align their risk tolerance with the inherent risks of each sector.

- *Low Risk, Low Return*: Sectors like residential or essential infrastructure may offer lower risk but correspondingly lower return potential. These sectors are often characterized by stable cash flows and long-term, predictable revenue streams.
- *Moderate Risk, Moderate Return*: Commercial and retail REITs may present a moderate level of risk and return. The performance of these sectors can be influenced by economic

conditions, tenant occupancy rates, and consumer trends. Investors comfortable with a balanced risk-return profile may find these sectors suitable.

- *Higher Risk, Higher Return*: Specialized or hybrid REITs, focusing on niche markets or combining multiple property types, can offer higher potential returns but come with increased risk. Investors seeking a more aggressive approach may consider these sectors, but they should be prepared for greater volatility.

Balancing risk and return is a crucial aspect of constructing a well-rounded REIT portfolio that aligns with your risk tolerance and investment goals.

2.7.3 Strategies for Diversification within REIT Types

Diversification is a fundamental principle of sound investment strategy, and it holds true within the realm of REITs. Investors can employ various strategies to diversify their REIT portfolio, spreading risk across different sectors and types.

- *Sector Diversification*: Allocate investments across different sectors of REITs to mitigate the impact of downturns in any specific market. A well-diversified portfolio may include residential, commercial, healthcare, and infrastructure REITs, among others.
- *Geographic Diversification*: Consider diversifying geographically to reduce exposure to regional economic fluctuations. Investing in REITs with properties in different regions or countries can enhance portfolio stability.
- *Risk-Return Diversification*: Balance higher-risk, higher-return investments with lower-risk, lower-return ones. For

example, combining income-focused REITs with growth-oriented or specialized REITs can provide a diversified portfolio with a range of risk-return profiles.

Diversification not only helps manage risk but also enhances the potential for long-term growth and stability. Carefully selecting a mix of REIT types and employing diversification strategies contribute to the resilience of a REIT portfolio in varying market conditions.

In conclusion, choosing the right type of REIT involves a thoughtful analysis of individual financial goals, risk tolerance, and the desire for income or capital appreciation. By aligning investments with specific objectives, balancing risk and return, and strategically diversifying within the REIT universe, investors can construct a portfolio that suits their unique preferences and positions them for long-term success in the dynamic real estate investment landscape.

Chapter 3: How REITs Work

Section 1: Structure of a REIT

Real Estate Investment Trusts (REITs) serve as a unique and accessible avenue for individuals to invest in real estate without the challenges of property ownership. In this section, we unravel the framework of REITs, exploring their corporate and trust structures, the roles of shareholders and the board of directors, and gaining an understanding of REIT management and operations.

Unraveling the Framework of Real Estate Investment Trusts

3.1.1 Corporate Structure vs. Trust Structure

One of the defining characteristics of REITs is their distinct structure, which can take on either a corporate or a trust form.

- *Corporate Structure*: Some REITs adopt a corporate structure, organizing themselves as standard corporations. In this model, the REIT issues shares of stock to investors, and the shareholders are considered partial owners of the corporation. The corporate structure provides flexibility in terms of management and operations and is subject to corporate income tax.
- *Trust Structure*: Alternatively, many REITs opt for a trust structure. In this setup, the REIT is akin to a trust, holding and managing real estate assets for the benefit of its shareholders. Investors purchase shares of the trust, and the

income generated from the real estate holdings is distributed to shareholders. Trust structures often enjoy certain tax advantages, as the income is typically not taxed at the corporate level, but instead, it flows through to shareholders.

The choice between a corporate or trust structure depends on factors such as tax considerations, operational preferences, and the nature of the real estate investments.

3.1.2 Shareholders and Board of Directors

A fundamental aspect of the REIT structure is the relationship between shareholders and the board of directors.

- *Shareholders*: Individuals who invest in a REIT become shareholders, holding shares that represent a proportional ownership interest in the real estate assets held by the REIT. Shareholders benefit from income generated by the REIT, primarily in the form of dividends. The ability to invest in shares makes REITs a liquid and accessible investment option for a broad range of investors.
- *Board of Directors*: The board of directors is responsible for overseeing the management and operations of the REIT. It is elected by the shareholders and acts in their best interests. The board makes key decisions, including the selection of the management team, approval of major transactions, and setting overall strategic direction. A well-functioning board is crucial for the governance and success of a REIT.

The relationship between shareholders and the board creates a governance structure that ensures transparency, accountability, and alignment of interests in the management of real estate assets.

3.1.3 Understanding REIT Management and Operations

The day-to-day management and operations of a REIT are handled by a team of professionals, including executives, property managers, and financial experts.

- *Executive Management*: The executive management team, led by a CEO or president, is responsible for the overall direction and performance of the REIT. This team makes strategic decisions, manages finances, and ensures the execution of the REIT's business plan. The effectiveness of the executive team is critical for achieving the financial goals of the REIT and delivering value to shareholders.
- *Property Management*: For REITs with direct ownership of properties, property management is a vital function. Property managers oversee the daily operations of real estate assets, including tenant relations, maintenance, and lease agreements. Effective property management contributes to the stability of rental income and the overall performance of the REIT's real estate portfolio.
- *Financial Management*: The financial team manages the REIT's finances, including budgeting, financial reporting, and compliance. Financial professionals play a crucial role in optimizing the REIT's financial performance, ensuring efficient use of capital, and maintaining compliance with regulatory requirements.

Understanding the roles and responsibilities of the management team provides investors with insights into the capabilities of the REIT in executing its business strategy.

In conclusion, the structure of a REIT is a carefully designed framework that balances the interests of shareholders, the responsibilities of the board of directors, and the expertise of the management team. Whether adopting a corporate or trust structure, REITs offer investors a way to participate in the real estate market without the challenges of direct property ownership. As we continue to explore the workings of REITs

Section 2: Legal Requirements and Tax Advantages

Navigating the legal landscape and understanding tax implications are critical aspects of Real Estate Investment Trusts (REITs). In this section, we delve into the legal requirements for maintaining REIT status, explore the tax advantages for both REITs and investors, examine the sources of qualifying income, and understand the implications of REIT tax pass-through status.

Navigating the Legal Landscape and Tax Implications of REITs

3.2.1 Compliance with IRS Requirements for REIT Status

Maintaining REIT status requires strict adherence to Internal Revenue Service (IRS) guidelines. To qualify as a REIT, entities must meet several criteria outlined in the Internal Revenue Code.

- *Asset Tests*: REITs must invest at least 75% of their total assets in real estate assets. These assets may include real property, cash, and government securities.
- *Income Tests*: At least 75% of a REIT's gross income must come from real estate-related sources, such as rents or

mortgage interest. Additionally, 95% of the REIT's income must be derived from qualifying sources, which include dividends, interest, and gains from the sale of real estate assets.

- *Distribution Requirements*: REITs are required to distribute at least 90% of their taxable income to shareholders in the form of dividends. This distribution serves to qualify for pass-through tax treatment and is a key feature that attracts income-seeking investors.
- *Shareholder Base*: REITs must have at least 100 shareholders and must not be excessively concentrated, with no five or fewer individuals owning more than 50% of the shares.

Compliance with these IRS requirements is essential for maintaining REIT status and enjoying the associated tax benefits.

3.2.2 Tax Advantages for REITs and Investors

REITs and investors alike benefit from the unique tax advantages offered by the structure.

- *No Corporate Income Tax*: One of the significant advantages is that REITs themselves are not subject to corporate income tax on the portion of their income distributed to shareholders as dividends. Instead, the tax obligation is shifted to the individual investors.
- *Pass-Through Taxation*: REITs operate as pass-through entities, meaning that their income is passed through to shareholders who report it on their individual tax returns. This pass-through structure avoids the double taxation typically associated with corporations, where income is taxed at both the corporate and individual levels.
- *Tax-Efficient Income*: The dividends distributed by REITs are

generally considered ordinary income for tax purposes. However, a portion of the dividends may qualify for the lower tax rates applicable to qualified dividends, offering tax efficiency for investors.

- *Tax Deferral through Like-Kind Exchanges*: REITs can engage in like-kind exchanges, deferring capital gains taxes when exchanging one real estate property for another. This tax deferral strategy allows REITs to optimize their real estate portfolios without triggering immediate tax liabilities.

3.2.3 Qualifying Income Sources for REITs

To maintain REIT status and enjoy tax advantages, a significant portion of a REIT's income must come from qualifying sources.

- *Rental Income*: Income generated from renting or leasing real property is a primary qualifying source for REITs. This includes rents from commercial, residential, and other types of real estate as discussed.
- *Interest Income*: REITs can earn interest income from loans secured by real estate. Mortgage-backed securities and other interest-bearing instruments related to real estate contribute to qualifying income.
- *Dividend Income*: Dividends received from other REITs and certain qualified real estate subsidiaries are considered qualifying income. This facilitates the creation of REIT portfolios with diversified income streams.
- *Capital Gains*: Gains from the sale or disposition of real estate assets contribute to a REIT's income. However, the 75% and 95% income tests impose limitations on the percentage of income derived from such gains.

Meeting these income requirements ensures that a REIT can maintain its tax-advantaged status and continue to provide attractive dividends to investors.

3.2.4 Implications of REIT Tax Pass-Through Status

The tax pass-through status of REITs has implications for both the entities and their investors.

- *Tax Treatment for REITs*: By distributing at least 90% of their taxable income to shareholders, REITs avoid corporate income tax. This allows more income to flow through to investors, making REITs an attractive investment option for those seeking regular income.
- *Tax Treatment for Investors*: Shareholders of REITs report their share of the REIT's income on their individual tax returns. The income is generally taxed at the individual's ordinary income tax rates. However, a portion of the dividends may qualify for the lower tax rates applicable to qualified dividends, providing potential tax advantages for investors.
- *Avoidance of Double Taxation*: The pass-through taxation structure ensures that income generated by the REIT is not taxed at both the corporate and individual levels, avoiding the double taxation commonly associated with traditional corporations.

Understanding the implications of REIT tax pass-through status allows both entities and investors to make informed decisions about participation in the REIT market.

In conclusion, the legal and tax framework surrounding REITs is a key aspect of their appeal to investors. By adhering to IRS requirements, REITs gain tax advantages that distinguish them from other investment vehicles. The pass-through taxation structure, coupled with the distribution requirements, contributes to the tax efficiency of REITs and makes them an attractive option for those seeking exposure to real estate with the added benefit of regular income.

Section 3: Income Streams: Dividends and Capital Gains

In the realm of Real Estate Investment Trusts (REITs), understanding the mechanisms of income generation is crucial for investors seeking both regular payouts and long-term growth. In this section, we explore the revenue generation aspects of REIT investments, focusing on the dividend distribution mechanism, the significance of Funds from Operations (FFO), the role of capital gains and appreciation, and the metrics of yield and total return.

Exploring Revenue Generation in REIT Investments

3.3.1 Dividend Distribution Mechanism

One of the primary attractions of investing in REITs is the consistent distribution of dividends. The dividend distribution mechanism is a fundamental aspect that aligns with the income-seeking objectives of many investors.

- *Regular Dividend Payouts*: REITs are required by law to distribute at least 90% of their taxable income to shareholders in the form of dividends. This consistent and predictable income stream appeals to investors seeking a steady source of passive income.

- *Monthly, Quarterly, or Annual Dividends*: The frequency of dividend distributions varies among REITs. Some may distribute dividends on a monthly basis, providing investors with more regular income, while others may opt for quarterly or annual distributions.
- *Tax Treatment of Dividends*: Dividends received from REITs are generally taxed at ordinary income tax rates. However, a portion of the dividends may qualify for the lower tax rates applicable to qualified dividends, offering potential tax advantages for investors.

The dividend distribution mechanism not only provides investors with a reliable income stream but also plays a crucial role in maintaining the tax-advantaged status of REITs.

3.3.2 Importance of FFO (Funds from Operations)

To gain a deeper understanding of a REIT's ability to sustain and grow dividends, investors often turn to Funds from Operations (FFO), a key financial metric specific to the real estate industry.

- *Calculation of FFO*: FFO represents the cash generated by a REIT's core operations. It is calculated by adding depreciation and amortization to earnings and subtracting gains or losses on the sale of properties. This adjustment accounts for the fact that depreciation is a non-cash expense.
- *Significance for Investors*: FFO provides a more accurate representation of a REIT's operating performance than traditional earnings. It helps investors assess the cash-generating capability of the REIT, which is crucial for sustaining dividend payments and supporting future growth.

- *Normalized FFO*: Some REITs also report Normalized Funds from Operations, which adjusts FFO for one-time or non-recurring items, providing a clearer picture of ongoing operational performance.

Investors often analyze FFO alongside other financial metrics to gauge the health and sustainability of a REIT's income stream.

3.3.3 Capital Gains and Appreciation in REITs

While dividends form a substantial part of the returns generated by REITs, capital gains and appreciation also play a crucial role in enhancing the overall value of a REIT investment.

- *Capital Gains from Property Sales*: REITs may realize capital gains through the sale of properties in their portfolio. When a property is sold at a profit, the capital gains contribute to the REIT's overall returns.
- *Share Price Appreciation*: Investors can also benefit from share price appreciation. As the value of the underlying real estate assets increases or as market conditions improve, the market price of the REIT's shares may rise, allowing investors to profit when they sell their shares.
- *Total Return Perspective*: Evaluating the total return of a REIT investment involves considering both dividend income and capital appreciation. This total return perspective provides a comprehensive view of the investment's performance over time.

3.3.4 Understanding Yield and Total Return in REIT Investments

Yield and total return are key metrics that investors use to assess the performance and attractiveness of REIT investments.

- *Yield*: The yield represents the income generated by a REIT as a percentage of its share price. It is calculated by dividing the annual dividends per share by the current market price per share. Yield is a critical metric for income-focused investors, providing insight into the level of income relative to the investment amount.
- *Total Return*: Total return encompasses both the income generated (dividends) and the capital appreciation of the investment. It provides a holistic measure of the overall performance of a REIT investment, considering both the income stream and the potential for the appreciation of the investment's value.

Understanding yield and total return allows investors to set realistic expectations and make informed decisions based on their financial goals and risk tolerance.

In conclusion, income generation in REIT investments is a multifaceted process that involves dividend distributions, the significance of Funds from Operations (FFO), and the potential for capital gains and appreciation. The dividend distribution mechanism serves as a cornerstone, providing investors with a reliable and regular income stream. FFO offers a deeper insight into the REIT's operating performance, and capital gains contribute to the overall returns of the investment. When investors consider yield and total return, they gain a comprehensive understanding of the income and growth potential of their REIT investments.

Section 4: Net Asset Value (NAV) and Share Price Dynamics

Analyzing the valuation and market performance of Real Estate Investment Trusts (REITs) involves delving into the Net Asset Value (NAV) and understanding the dynamics that influence share prices. In this section, we explore the calculation of Net Asset Value, the factors influencing share prices, the role of market perception and investor sentiment, and the impact of real estate market cycles on REITs.

Analyzing the Valuation and Market Performance of REITs

3.4.1 Calculating Net Asset Value (NAV) in REITs

Net Asset Value (NAV) is a critical metric that provides insight into the intrinsic value of a REIT. Calculating NAV involves assessing the value of the REIT's assets and subtracting its liabilities, resulting in the net value of the real estate holdings.

- *Asset Valuation*: Determining the value of real estate assets involves appraising properties to reflect their current market value. The appraisals may consider factors such as location, property condition, and income potential.
- *Liability Assessment*: Liabilities, including debt obligations and operational expenses, are subtracted from the total asset value to arrive at the Net Asset Value.
- *Per-Share NAV*: The per-share NAV is calculated by dividing the total NAV by the number of outstanding shares. This figure provides a measure of the net value of a REIT on a per-share basis.

Analyzing NAV allows investors to assess whether a REIT's shares are trading at a premium or discount to their intrinsic value.

3.4.2 Factors Influencing Share Prices

Understanding the dynamics that influence share prices is crucial for investors seeking to make informed decisions in the REIT market.

- *Dividend Yield*: The dividend yield, calculated as the annual dividend per share divided by the share price, is a key factor influencing investor interest. A higher dividend yield relative to other investment options may attract income-focused investors.
- *Funds from Operations (FFO)*: FFO, which reflects the cash generated by a REIT's operations, can impact share prices. Positive FFO growth and stability can contribute to a positive perception of the REIT's financial health.
- *Interest Rates*: Interest rates play a significant role in the valuation of income-generating assets, including real estate. When interest rates rise, the appeal of dividend-paying investments like REITs may diminish, affecting share prices.
- *Economic Conditions*: The overall economic environment can influence the performance of REITs. Economic growth, employment rates, and consumer spending impact the demand for different types of real estate, influencing the revenue potential of REITs.
- *Market Sentiment*: Investor perception and sentiment can drive share prices. Positive news about a REIT's performance, strategic initiatives, or the real estate market in general can attract investors, leading to an increase in share prices.

3.4.3 Market Perception and Investor Sentiment

Market perception and investor sentiment can have a profound impact on the performance of REITs. The market's view of a REIT's potential for growth, stability, and income generation can influence buying and selling decisions.

- *Positive Sentiment*: Positive news such as strong financial results, successful property acquisitions, or favorable market conditions can boost investor confidence. Positive sentiment often leads to increased demand for shares, potentially driving up prices.
- *Negative Sentiment*: Conversely, negative news, economic uncertainties, or poor financial performance may result in a decline in investor confidence. Negative sentiment can lead to selling pressure, impacting share prices.
- *Long-Term vs. Short-Term Sentiment*: It's essential for investors to distinguish between short-term market fluctuations driven by sentiment and the long-term fundamentals of a REIT. While short-term sentiment can impact share prices, a focus on the underlying financial health and strategic vision of the REIT is crucial for long-term investors.

3.4.4 Real Estate Market Cycles and their Impact on REITs

Real estate markets often go through cycles influenced by factors such as economic conditions, interest rates, and supply and demand dynamics. Understanding these cycles is essential for evaluating the potential impact on REITs.

- *Expansion Phase*: During an expansion phase, characterized

by economic growth and increased demand for real estate, REITs may experience rising property values and rental income. Share prices may respond positively during this phase.
- *Contraction Phase*: Economic downturns or market corrections can lead to a contraction phase. During this period, REITs may face challenges such as lower occupancy rates and declining property values, potentially impacting share prices.
- *Recovery Phase*: As the real estate market rebounds from a contraction, REITs may benefit from improving property values and increased demand. Investors may regain confidence, positively impacting share prices.
- *Stable Phase*: In stable market conditions, REITs may experience consistent performance with steady rental income and property values. Investors seeking stable income may find these periods attractive.

Understanding the dynamics of real estate market cycles allows investors to anticipate potential challenges and opportunities, guiding their decision-making in different market environments.

In conclusion, analyzing the valuation and market performance of REITs involves a multifaceted approach that considers Net Asset Value (NAV), factors influencing share prices, market perception, and the impact of real estate market cycles. NAV provides a fundamental measure of a REIT's intrinsic value, while factors like dividend yield, FFO, and economic conditions influence investor interest. Market sentiment, both positive and negative, can drive short-term price movements, and an awareness of real estate market cycles helps investors navigate varying market conditions.

Chapter 4: Assessing Risks in REIT Investing

Section 1: Market Risks

Investing in Real Estate Investment Trusts (REITs) comes with inherent risks, and understanding these risks is crucial for making informed investment decisions. In this section, we delve into market risks, exploring the impact of market dynamics on REITs, the relationship between REITs and broader market trends, and the influence of investor sentiment and market speculation.

Understanding the Impact of Market Dynamics on REITs

4.1.1 Market Volatility and REIT Performance

Market volatility is a fundamental aspect that can significantly impact the performance of REITs. REITs, like other publicly traded securities, are influenced by the ebb and flow of market sentiment, economic conditions, and geopolitical events.

- *Sensitivity to Interest Rates*: REITs are often sensitive to changes in interest rates. When interest rates rise, the appeal of dividend-paying investments like REITs may diminish, leading to potential selling pressure and a decline in share prices. Conversely, during periods of declining interest rates, REITs may experience increased demand.
- *Economic Uncertainty*: Economic uncertainties, such as recessions or global financial crises, can create market volatility. During these periods, the demand for various types

of real estate may be affected, impacting the rental income and property values of REITs.

- *Market Corrections and Downturns*: Market corrections or downturns can lead to a broad sell-off across various asset classes, including REITs. Investors may seek to reallocate their portfolios, and REITs can experience declines even if the underlying real estate fundamentals remain sound.

Investors should be mindful of market volatility and consider their risk tolerance and investment horizon when incorporating REITs into their portfolios.

4.1.2 Relationship Between REITs and Broader Market Trends

The relationship between REITs and broader market trends is complex, and various factors can influence how REITs respond to overall market conditions.

- *Cyclical Nature of Real Estate*: Real estate is inherently cyclical, with periods of expansion, contraction, and stability. The broader economic cycle and real estate market trends can impact the performance of different types of REITs.
- *Correlation with Equities*: While REITs are often considered an alternative asset class, their correlation with equities can vary. During periods of economic growth, REITs may exhibit positive correlation with the stock market. However, during economic downturns, they may demonstrate diversification benefits as income-generating assets.
- *Flight to Safety*: In times of economic uncertainty or market stress, investors may seek "safe-haven" assets. REITs, particularly those with a focus on stable income-producing properties, can be perceived as defensive investments,

potentially attracting capital during turbulent market conditions.

Investors should be aware of the relationship between REITs and broader market trends to make strategic investment decisions aligned with their financial objectives.

4.1.3 Investor Sentiment and Market Speculation

Investor sentiment and market speculation play a significant role in shaping short-term movements in REIT prices. These factors can create opportunities but also introduce risks for investors.

- *Positive Sentiment*: Positive sentiment, driven by favorable economic indicators, strong real estate market conditions, or positive news about specific REITs, can lead to increased demand and higher share prices. However, relying solely on positive sentiment without considering underlying fundamentals can expose investors to potential market exuberance.
- *Negative Sentiment*: Conversely, negative sentiment, often fueled by economic concerns, global events, or negative news about the real estate sector, can lead to selling pressure and declines in REIT prices. Investors should be cautious about market panics and evaluate the long-term fundamentals of the REITs they hold.
- *Market Speculation*: Speculative trading can contribute to short-term volatility in REIT prices. Investors engaging in speculative behavior may contribute to exaggerated price movements that are not necessarily aligned with the underlying value of the real estate assets.

Investors should approach market sentiment and speculation with a discerning eye, focusing on the fundamental strength and long-term prospects of the REITs in their portfolio.

In conclusion, market risks are inherent in REIT investing, and understanding the impact of market dynamics is essential for managing these risks effectively. Market volatility, the relationship between REITs and broader market trends, and the influence of investor sentiment and speculation all contribute to the risk landscape. While market conditions can create challenges, they also present opportunities for investors to build diversified and resilient portfolios.

Section 2: Interest Rate Risks

Interest rate risks are a critical consideration for investors in Real Estate Investment Trusts (REITs), as these risks can have a profound impact on the performance of the asset class. In this section, we delve into the sensitivity of REITs to changes in interest rates, exploring the relationship between interest rates and real estate financing, the impact of rising and falling interest rates on REITs, and the concepts of yield compression and spread risk.

Analyzing the Sensitivity of REITs to Interest Rate Changes

4.2.1 Interest Rates and Real Estate Financing

The connection between interest rates and real estate financing is integral to understanding how changes in interest rates can influence the performance of REITs.

- *Cost of Borrowing*: REITs often rely on debt to finance property acquisitions and expansions. The cost of borrowing for REITs is influenced by prevailing interest rates. When interest rates are low, REITs can secure financing at more favorable terms, enhancing their ability to undertake new projects and increase property holdings.

- *Capitalization Rates*: Changes in interest rates can impact capitalization rates, which are fundamental to real estate valuation. As interest rates rise, capitalization rates may increase, potentially leading to lower property valuations. Conversely, falling interest rates may result in lower capitalization rates, potentially boosting property values.
- *Refinancing Risks*: REITs with existing debt may face challenges when refinancing in a rising interest rate environment. Higher interest rates can lead to increased borrowing costs, affecting the profitability of existing projects and potentially limiting the REIT's ability to pursue new opportunities.

Understanding the intricacies of interest rate movements and their impact on real estate financing is crucial for investors seeking to navigate the dynamic landscape of REITs.

4.2.2 Impact of Rising and Falling Interest Rates on REITs

The direction of interest rate movements—whether rising or falling—can have distinct implications for REIT performance.

- *Rising Interest Rates*: When interest rates rise, REITs may face several challenges. The cost of debt increases, potentially reducing profitability. Higher interest rates may lead to a decrease in property values, affecting the overall portfolio valuation. Investors may also shift their preferences toward other income-generating investments with potentially higher yields.

- *Falling Interest Rates*: Conversely, falling interest rates can present opportunities for REITs. The cost of borrowing decreases, making it more affordable for REITs to finance projects and expand their portfolios. Lower interest rates may also contribute to higher property valuations, benefiting existing holdings. Additionally, the relative attractiveness of REIT dividends may increase when compared to other income-generating investments.

Investors should monitor interest rate trends and assess their potential impact on the broader economy and real estate market when making decisions about REIT investments.

4.2.3 Yield Compression and Spread Risk

Yield compression and spread risk are concepts closely tied to interest rate movements and can significantly impact the performance of REITs.

- *Yield Compression*: Yield compression occurs when the spread between the capitalization rate and the risk-free rate narrows. In other words, as interest rates decline, the potential yield from real estate investments may decrease. This can affect the attractiveness of REITs, particularly for income-focused investors, as the relative yield compared to other investments may diminish.
- *Spread Risk*: Spread risk refers to the vulnerability of REITs to changes in the yield spread between their income-generating assets and the risk-free rate. When the spread widens, indicating a higher potential return relative to the risk-free rate, REITs may become more appealing. Conversely, if the

spread narrows, it can reduce the relative attractiveness of REITs.

Investors should carefully assess the yield environment and the potential for yield compression when evaluating the risk-return profile of REIT investments.

In conclusion, interest rate risks are a significant consideration for investors in REITs, given the close relationship between interest rates and real estate financing. The cost of borrowing, capitalization rates, and the ability to refinance debt are all influenced by changes in interest rates. The impact of rising and falling interest rates on REITs can be multifaceted, presenting challenges and opportunities depending on the prevailing economic conditions. Additionally, concepts such as yield compression and spread risk highlight the importance of monitoring yield dynamics in the context of interest rate movements.

Section 3: Property-Specific Risks

In the realm of Real Estate Investment Trusts (REITs), understanding and evaluating risks at the property level is essential for informed decision-making. This section delves into the nuanced landscape of property-specific risks, addressing factors such as location-specific considerations, property management risks, market demand, competition, and tenant-related considerations.

4.3.1 Location-Specific Factors

Location is a cornerstone of real estate, and the success of a property within a REIT portfolio is intricately tied to its geographic context. Various location-specific factors can significantly impact the risk profile of a property.

Accessibility and Infrastructure: The accessibility and quality of local infrastructure, including transportation networks and utilities, influence a property's desirability. Proximity to highways, public transportation, and essential services can enhance a property's appeal and market value.

Economic Stability: The economic health of the region in which a property is situated plays a pivotal role. Local economic conditions, job markets, and the overall business environment can affect property values and rental income. Investing in areas with diverse and resilient economies can mitigate risks associated with economic downturns.

Regulatory Environment: The regulatory landscape varies across regions and can impact property development, land use, and zoning. Investors must navigate local regulations to anticipate potential hurdles or opportunities tied to specific locations.

Natural and Climate Risks: Properties in regions prone to natural disasters, such as earthquakes, floods, or hurricanes, carry inherent risks. Evaluating the susceptibility of a property to these events is crucial for risk assessment and implementing mitigation strategies.

4.3.2 Property Management Risks

Efficient property management is critical for optimizing returns and minimizing risks. Property management risks can stem from various operational aspects that impact a property's performance.

Maintenance and Repairs: Inadequate maintenance can lead to the depreciation of property value and increased operational costs. Regular assessments of a property's condition and proactive maintenance measures are vital for mitigating this risk.

Tenant Relations: Effective property management involves maintaining positive relationships with tenants. Tenant turnover, disputes, or non-compliance with lease agreements can pose risks. Property managers must employ strategies to foster positive tenant relations and address issues promptly.

Operational Efficiency: Inefficient property management practices can result in higher operational costs and reduced profitability. Implementing streamlined and cost-effective management processes is crucial for mitigating operational risks.

4.3.3 Market Demand and Competition

Understanding the local market dynamics is essential for assessing the demand for a property and anticipating potential competition.

Market Demand: Changes in demographic trends, population growth, and shifts in consumer behavior can impact the demand for certain types of properties. Anticipating these changes allows REITs to adjust their portfolios accordingly.

Competition from New Developments: The introduction of new properties in the market can intensify competition. Assessing the pipeline of upcoming developments in a particular area helps REITs understand potential challenges to occupancy rates and rental prices.

4.3.4 Tenant Risk and Lease Terms

The stability and reliability of tenants significantly influence a property's income stream. Evaluating tenant-related risks involves assessing factors such as lease terms, tenant creditworthiness, and the diversity of tenants within a property.

Lease Expirations and Renewals: Concentration of lease expirations within a short timeframe can expose a property to vacancy risks. A well-diversified lease expiration schedule and proactive lease renewal strategies are essential for mitigating this risk.

Tenant Credit Quality: Assessing the creditworthiness of tenants is crucial. A diverse tenant base with reputable and financially stable occupants reduces the risk of income disruption due to defaults.

Lease Terms and Conditions: The terms and conditions outlined in leases, such as rent escalation clauses and tenant responsibilities, impact a property's financial performance. Understanding and negotiating favorable lease terms is integral to risk management.

In conclusion, property-specific risks in REIT investing demand a comprehensive evaluation of location-specific factors, efficient property management practices, awareness of market demand and competition, and a keen understanding of tenant-related considerations. Successful risk management at the property level involves a proactive and informed approach, combining thorough due diligence with strategic decision-making. REITs that navigate and mitigate property-specific risks effectively position themselves for sustainable long-term growth and resilience in the dynamic real estate landscape.

Section 4: Economic Downturns and REITs

Economic downturns pose challenges to various sectors, and real estate, including Real Estate Investment Trusts (REITs), is not immune to the impacts of economic recessions. This section explores the resilience of REITs during economic challenges, delving into their historical performance, sensitivity to economic indicators, and the broader impact of global economic factors.

4.4.1 Historical Performance During Economic Recessions

One of the key aspects of assessing the resilience of REITs during economic downturns is examining their historical performance. REITs have demonstrated a mixed but generally resilient track record during periods of economic contraction.

Real Estate as a Defensive Asset: While equity markets often experience significant volatility during economic downturns, real estate, including REITs, has been considered a defensive asset class. The tangible nature of real estate, coupled with the steady income generated from leases, can provide a level of stability compared to more volatile investment options.

Diversification Benefits: The performance of REITs during economic downturns is influenced by factors such as the property types within their portfolios. Diversified REITs, with exposure to various sectors like healthcare, residential, and infrastructure, have historically shown greater resilience. The income generated from different property types can act as a stabilizing factor during economic uncertainties.

Impact on Property Values: Economic recessions may lead to declines in property values, affecting the net asset value (NAV) of REITs. However, the long-term nature of real estate investments often means that property values can recover as economic conditions improve. Investors in REITs with strong fundamentals may view downturns as opportunities to acquire assets at discounted prices.

4.4.2 Sensitivity to Economic Indicators

REITs are sensitive to various economic indicators that reflect the health of the broader economy. Understanding these indicators is crucial for assessing how REITs might perform during economic downturns.

Interest Rates: Changes in interest rates can significantly impact the cost of financing for real estate projects. During economic downturns, central banks may implement lower interest rates to stimulate economic activity. While lower rates can reduce borrowing costs for REITs, they may also reflect challenging economic conditions.

Employment and Consumer Spending: Economic recessions often result in rising unemployment and reduced consumer spending. This can affect various sectors of real estate, such as retail and commercial properties, as businesses may face lower demand and consumers curtail discretionary spending. Residential REITs, on the other hand, might experience increased demand for rental properties if homeownership becomes less accessible.

Housing Market Dynamics: Economic downturns can impact the housing market, influencing both residential and commercial real estate. Residential REITs may be affected by shifts in demand for rental properties, while commercial REITs may experience changes in office space demand as businesses reassess their spatial needs.

4.4.3 Impact of Global Economic Factors on REITs

The interconnectedness of global economies means that REITs can be influenced by economic factors beyond national borders. Understanding the global economic landscape is crucial for assessing the potential impact on REITs during economic downturns.

Globalization and International Investments: Some REITs have expanded their portfolios to include international properties. While this provides diversification benefits, it also exposes them to global economic conditions. Economic downturns in one region can influence the performance of international real estate holdings.

Currency Exchange Rates: REITs with international exposure may face challenges related to currency exchange rates. Economic downturns can lead to fluctuations in currency values, impacting the translation of international earnings into the REIT's reporting currency.

Trade and Supply Chain Disruptions: Economic recessions can lead to disruptions in global trade and supply chains. This can impact sectors such as industrial and logistics properties, affecting the performance of REITs with exposure to these segments.

In conclusion, assessing the resilience of REITs during economic downturns requires a comprehensive understanding of historical performance, sensitivity to economic indicators, and the impact of global economic factors. While REITs have demonstrated resilience in various economic climates, investors must remain vigilant, considering the dynamic nature of real estate markets and their sensitivity to broader economic trends. Thorough due diligence, diversification, and a long-term investment perspective are key elements in navigating the complexities of economic downturns within the REIT landscape.

Section 5: Mitigating Risks Through Diversification

Real Estate Investment Trusts (REITs) provide investors with exposure to the real estate market, offering the potential for steady income and capital appreciation. However, like any investment, REITs come with inherent risks. This section delves into strategic approaches to enhance risk management in REIT portfolios, emphasizing the importance of diversification, balancing property types and geographical exposure, incorporating different risk profiles in REIT selection, and the necessity of regular portfolio review and adjustment for effective risk mitigation.

4.5.1 Importance of Diversification

Diversification Fundamentals: Diversification is a cornerstone of risk management in any investment strategy, and it holds particular significance in the realm of REITs. By spreading investments across various assets, such as different types of properties and sectors, investors can reduce exposure to the risks associated with any single investment. Diversification is a powerful tool that can enhance portfolio stability.

Property Type Diversification: REITs cover a broad spectrum of property types, including residential, commercial, healthcare, and infrastructure. Each property type responds differently to economic conditions and market cycles. By diversifying across these categories, investors can mitigate risks associated with the performance of a specific property sector. For example, during economic downturns, residential properties may maintain stability, while commercial properties might experience challenges.

Sector and Industry Exposure: Within the commercial real estate sector, there are various industries such as office spaces, retail, and industrial properties. Diversifying across these industries can provide an additional layer of risk mitigation. For instance, if one sector faces challenges, others may remain resilient, contributing to the overall stability of the REIT portfolio.

4.5.2 Balancing Property Types and Geographical Exposure

Geographical Diversification: Beyond diversification based on property types, geographical diversification is equally important. Real estate markets can vary significantly from one region to another due to factors such as economic conditions, population growth, and local market dynamics. By investing in REITs with properties in different regions, investors can reduce the impact of regional economic downturns and take advantage of growth opportunities in diverse markets.

Balancing Risk and Return: The quest for optimal risk-adjusted returns involves striking a balance between risk and potential rewards. While some regions or property types may offer higher returns, they often come with increased risk. Balancing a REIT portfolio involves careful consideration of the risk-return profile of each investment, ensuring that the overall portfolio aligns with the investor's risk tolerance and financial goals.

4.5.3 Incorporating Different Risk Profiles in REIT Selection

Core, Value-Add, and Opportunistic Strategies: REITs adopt different strategies when managing their portfolios. Understanding these strategies is crucial for investors seeking to diversify based on risk profiles. Core REITs typically focus on stable, income-generating properties, offering lower risk but potentially lower returns. Value-add and opportunistic REITs, on the other hand, may pursue higher-risk projects with the potential for greater returns. A well-diversified portfolio may include a mix of these strategies to balance risk and reward.

4.5.4 Regular Portfolio Review and Adjustment for Risk Mitigation

Dynamic Nature of Real Estate Markets: Real estate markets are dynamic and subject to changing economic conditions. Regular portfolio reviews are essential to adapt to evolving market trends and mitigate emerging risks. Investors should stay informed about economic indicators, interest rate movements, and changes in property market dynamics. Adjustments to the portfolio may involve rebalancing allocations, exiting underperforming assets, or reallocating resources based on emerging opportunities.

Utilizing Technology and Research: In the digital age, technology provides investors with advanced tools for portfolio analysis. Utilizing data analytics, investors can monitor the performance of individual REITs, assess market trends, and make informed decisions. Additionally, staying abreast of industry research, market reports, and economic forecasts enhances the ability to identify potential risks and opportunities, supporting effective risk management.

Conclusion

Mitigating risks through diversification is a fundamental principle in managing a successful REIT portfolio. By embracing a diversified approach that encompasses different property types, geographical regions, and risk profiles, investors can enhance the resilience of their portfolios. Regular portfolio reviews, staying informed about market dynamics, and leveraging technological tools contribute to a proactive risk management strategy. In the dynamic landscape of real estate investing, diversification stands as a robust shield against uncertainties, providing investors with a balanced and resilient foundation for long-term success.

Chapter 5: Getting Started with REIT Investing

Section 1: Setting Investment Goals

Investing in Real Estate Investment Trusts (REITs) requires a strategic approach that begins with setting clear investment goals. In this section, we explore the importance of defining your financial objectives in REIT investing, considering factors such as the timeline of goals, the balance between income generation and capital appreciation, and aligning REIT investments with your overall financial plan.

Defining Your Financial Objectives in REIT Investing

Investors embark on the journey of REIT investing with diverse financial objectives. Whether seeking regular income, long-term growth, or a combination of both, clarifying these objectives is fundamental to constructing a well-rounded and purposeful REIT portfolio.

5.1.1 Short-Term vs. Long-Term Goals

Understanding the time horizon of your investment goals is a cornerstone of effective REIT investing. Short-term goals may involve generating immediate income or capitalizing on specific market trends, while long-term goals often encompass wealth accumulation, retirement planning, or funding major life events.

- *Short-Term Goals*: Investors with short-term goals may

prioritize immediate income needs, such as supplemental monthly cash flow or funding short-term financial objectives. This could involve focusing on REITs with high dividend yields or those positioned to benefit from short-term market trends.

- *Long-Term Goals*: For investors with a longer time horizon, such as those planning for retirement or wealth accumulation over decades, a more diversified and growth-oriented approach may be appropriate. Long-term investors can afford to weather market fluctuations and benefit from the compounding effects of reinvested dividends.

5.1.2 Income Generation vs. Capital Appreciation

One of the key decisions in setting investment goals for REITs is determining the balance between income generation and capital appreciation.

- *Income Generation*: Some investors prioritize regular income streams and consistent dividends. This approach is well-suited for those seeking passive income to support living expenses or supplement other sources of revenue.
- *Capital Appreciation*: Alternatively, investors may focus on the potential for capital appreciation, anticipating growth in the value of their REIT holdings over time. This strategy is aligned with a belief in the appreciation of real estate values and may suit those with a longer investment horizon.

5.1.3 Aligning REIT Investments with Overall Financial Plan

Setting investment goals within the context of an overall financial plan ensures that REIT investments contribute cohesively to your broader wealth management strategy.

- *Risk Tolerance and Asset Allocation*: Consider your risk tolerance and how REITs fit into your overall asset allocation. Different types of REITs carry varying levels of risk, and aligning these with your risk tolerance is critical for a well-balanced portfolio.
- *Diversification*: Ensure that your REIT investments complement other assets in your portfolio, providing diversification benefits. A diversified portfolio can help mitigate specific risks associated with individual REITs or real estate sectors.
- *Tax Considerations*: Understand the tax implications of REIT investments and how they align with your overall tax strategy. REIT dividends, for example, are often taxed differently than traditional equity dividends.

By aligning your REIT investments with your broader financial plan, you create a roadmap that integrates these assets into your wealth-building strategy.

In conclusion, setting investment goals is the foundational step in REIT investing. Whether aiming for short-term income, long-term growth, or a balanced combination of both, clarity on your financial objectives guides subsequent decisions in constructing and managing your REIT portfolio. The balance between income generation and capital appreciation should reflect your risk tolerance and time horizon, while alignment with your overall financial plan ensures a cohesive and purposeful approach to REIT investing.

Section 2: Understanding Your Risk Tolerance

Real Estate Investment Trusts (REITs) offer an avenue for investors to participate in the real estate market without directly owning properties. However, like all investments, REITs come with a degree of risk. Understanding and managing risk is a critical aspect of successful investing. This section explores the importance of assessing and managing risk in REIT investments, utilizing risk assessment tools, identifying personal risk tolerance, and achieving a balance between risk and reward within REIT portfolios.

5.2.1 Risk Assessment Tools and Questionnaires

Importance of Systematic Risk Evaluation: Before delving into the world of REIT investments, it's crucial for investors to conduct a comprehensive risk assessment. Numerous tools and questionnaires are available to assist in this process. These tools are designed to evaluate an individual's risk appetite, financial goals, and investment horizon. By systematically assessing risk factors, investors can make informed decisions aligned with their overall financial strategy.

Risk Tolerance Questionnaires: Risk tolerance questionnaires are valuable instruments commonly used by financial advisors and investment platforms. These questionnaires typically present investors with a series of scenarios and ask them to choose their comfort level with different risk levels. Questions may cover aspects such as investment goals, time horizon, and reactions to market fluctuations. The analysis of responses helps to quantify an individual's risk tolerance, providing a baseline for constructing a suitable investment portfolio.

Customized Risk Tools: Some financial institutions and investment platforms provide customized risk assessment tools tailored to specific investment products, including REITs. These tools consider factors such as the investor's knowledge about REITs, previous investment experience, and preferences regarding income generation versus capital appreciation. Utilizing these tools can enhance the precision of risk assessment and help investors align their portfolios with their unique financial circumstances.

5.2.2 Identifying Personal Risk Tolerance

Understanding Risk Tolerance: Risk tolerance refers to an investor's ability to endure fluctuations in the value of their investments and still stay committed to their long-term financial objectives. Identifying one's risk tolerance is a personal and subjective process influenced by factors such as financial goals, time horizon, and emotional disposition towards market volatility.

Balancing Objectives and Risk Tolerance: Investors need to strike a balance between their financial objectives and risk tolerance. Conservative investors may prioritize capital preservation and steady income, leading them to favor lower-risk REITs focused on stable, income-generating properties. Conversely, aggressive investors with a higher risk tolerance may seek higher returns by investing in growth-oriented REITs or those involved in development projects.

5.2.3 Balancing Risk and Reward in REIT Portfolios

Risk-Return Relationship: The relationship between risk and return is a fundamental concept in investing. Generally, higher returns come with higher risks, and finding the right balance is essential. In the context of REIT portfolios, investors must evaluate their risk tolerance in conjunction with their return expectations.

Diversification as a Risk Management Strategy: Diversification is a powerful tool to balance risk and reward in REIT portfolios. By spreading investments across different types of REITs, geographical regions, and property sectors, investors can reduce the impact of poor performance in any single investment. Diversification serves as a risk mitigation strategy, particularly during market fluctuations and economic uncertainties.

Understanding REIT Risk Factors: Different types of REITs carry distinct risk factors. For example, residential REITs may be influenced by housing market dynamics, while retail REITs may face challenges from shifts in consumer behavior. Understanding these specific risks enables investors to make informed decisions about the composition of their portfolios.

Periodic Review and Adjustment: Risk tolerance is not static; it can evolve over time due to changes in financial circumstances, personal goals, or market conditions. Regularly reviewing and reassessing one's risk tolerance is crucial. Additionally, adjustments to the REIT portfolio may be necessary to align with any changes in risk appetite. This periodic review ensures that the portfolio remains in line with the investor's evolving financial strategy.

Conclusion

Understanding and managing risk is integral to successful REIT investing. Through the use of risk assessment tools, investors can gain insights into their risk tolerance and align their investments with their financial goals. Striking a balance between risk and reward is an ongoing process that involves continuous evaluation, diversification, and periodic adjustments. By navigating these considerations thoughtfully, investors can build and maintain a REIT portfolio that reflects their risk preferences and positions them for long-term financial success.

Section 3: Building a REIT Investment Portfolio

Constructing a robust and effective REIT investment portfolio involves careful consideration of various factors. In this section, we explore the essential elements of building a diversified and balanced REIT portfolio, including asset allocation strategies, the importance of diversification across REIT types, and considerations for portfolio size and position sizing.

Constructing a Diversified and Balanced REIT Portfolio

Building a REIT portfolio is akin to crafting a well-structured and resilient investment strategy. By understanding the nuances of asset allocation, diversification, and portfolio size, investors can optimize their exposure to the real estate market while managing risk effectively.

5.3.1 Asset Allocation Strategies

Asset allocation is a key element of portfolio construction, defining the proportion of your investment portfolio dedicated to different asset classes, including REITs. Various asset allocation strategies exist, each catering to different risk appetites and investment goals.

- *Strategic Asset Allocation*: This approach involves setting a predetermined, long-term allocation to different asset classes based on the investor's risk tolerance and financial objectives. Strategic asset allocation aims to maintain a consistent balance over time, adjusting periodically as financial goals evolve.
- *Tactical Asset Allocation*: Investors employing tactical asset

allocation make short-term adjustments to their portfolio based on perceived market opportunities or risks. This approach allows for flexibility in responding to changing market conditions, potentially capitalizing on short-term trends.

- *Dynamic Asset Allocation*: Dynamic asset allocation combines elements of both strategic and tactical approaches. It involves periodically reassessing the portfolio's strategic asset allocation based on prevailing market conditions and adjusting allocations accordingly.

Selecting an asset allocation strategy depends on factors such as investment horizon, risk tolerance, and market outlook. While strategic asset allocation provides a disciplined, long-term approach, tactical and dynamic approaches may be suitable for investors comfortable with more frequent adjustments.

5.3.2 Importance of Diversification Across REIT Types

As discussed, diversification is a fundamental principle in portfolio management, and it holds particular significance in the context of REIT investments. Diversifying across different types of REITs helps mitigate risks associated with specific sectors or property types.

- *Residential REITs*: These focus on apartment buildings and multi-family properties. They are influenced by factors such as population growth, rental demand, and regional housing trends.
- *Commercial REITs*: These include office buildings, retail spaces, and industrial properties. Performance is tied to economic conditions, corporate demand for office space, and retail trends.

- *Retail REITs*: Investments in malls, shopping centers, and individual retail properties. Performance is influenced by consumer spending habits, e-commerce trends, and the overall retail landscape.
- *Healthcare REITs*: Specializing in properties such as hospitals, medical offices, and senior living facilities. Performance is linked to demographic trends and healthcare industry dynamics.
- *Infrastructure REITs*: Focused on essential infrastructure assets such as energy, utilities, and communication infrastructure. Performance is influenced by long-term stability and the demand for critical services.
- *Specialized and Hybrid REITs*: These include special-purpose REITs, such as those focused on data centers or timber, and hybrid REITs that combine multiple property types. Performance depends on the specific characteristics of the chosen niche.

Diversification across these types of REITs helps spread risk and capture opportunities in different segments of the real estate market. Investors should consider their risk tolerance and investment goals when determining the optimal mix of REIT types in their portfolio.

5.3.3 Portfolio Size and Position Sizing

The size of your REIT investment portfolio and the allocation to individual REITs within the portfolio are critical considerations. Proper position sizing ensures that no single investment has an undue impact on the overall portfolio performance.

- *Portfolio Size*: The total size of your investment portfolio, including REITs and other asset classes, should align with your overall financial plan and risk tolerance. Larger portfolios may afford greater diversification opportunities and potential for risk mitigation.

- *Position Sizing*: The allocation of funds to individual REITs within the portfolio is equally crucial. Position sizing involves determining what percentage of the portfolio each REIT should represent. This decision should consider factors such as the risk-return profile of each REIT, market conditions, and the investor's overall risk tolerance.
- *Risk Management*: Diversification and position sizing contribute to effective risk management. Avoiding over-concentration in a single REIT or sector helps mitigate the impact of adverse events on the overall portfolio. Investors should regularly review and adjust position sizes based on changes in market conditions and individual REIT performance.

In conclusion, constructing a diversified and balanced REIT portfolio is a nuanced process that involves strategic asset allocation, diversification across different types of REITs, and thoughtful consideration of portfolio size and position sizing. Asset allocation strategies should align with the investor's risk tolerance and financial goals, while diversification across residential, commercial, retail, healthcare, infrastructure, and specialized REITs helps spread risk and capture opportunities in diverse real estate segments. Portfolio size and position sizing are critical for effective risk management, ensuring that the impact of individual REITs on the overall portfolio remains proportionate.

Section 4: Researching and Selecting REITs

Researching and selecting Real Estate Investment Trusts (REITs) requires a comprehensive approach that goes beyond surface-level analysis. In this section, we explore the intricacies of conducting due diligence in the REIT market, including fundamental analysis, reading financial statements and key metrics, analyzing management teams and track records, and utilizing research tools and resources for effective REIT selection.

Conducting Due Diligence in the REIT Market

Due diligence is a crucial step in the process of investing in REITs. It involves thorough research and analysis to gain a deep understanding of the fundamental aspects that drive the performance of a REIT. By employing a systematic approach to due diligence, investors can make informed decisions and build a well-constructed REIT portfolio.

5.4.1 Fundamental Analysis of REITs

Fundamental analysis is the cornerstone of evaluating the financial health and performance potential of REITs. This analysis involves assessing various qualitative and quantitative factors.

- *Market Conditions*: Understand the broader economic and real estate market conditions. Consider factors such as interest rates, demographic trends, and regional economic indicators, as they directly impact the performance of different types of REITs.
- *Property Portfolio*: Evaluate the quality, location, and diversity of a REIT's property portfolio. Assess the demand and outlook for the specific types of real estate in which the REIT invests. Consider the geographical distribution of properties

to ensure a well-diversified portfolio.

- *Occupancy Rates and Lease Terms*: Examine the occupancy rates and lease terms of the properties in the REIT's portfolio. High occupancy rates and favorable lease terms contribute to stable rental income and overall financial health.

5.4.2 Reading Financial Statements and Key Metrics

Understanding the financial statements and key metrics of a REIT is essential for evaluating its financial stability and growth potential.

- *Revenue and Net Operating Income (NOI)*: Analyze the revenue and NOI to assess the income-generating capacity of the REIT. Consistent growth in these metrics indicates financial stability and potential for dividend growth.
- *Funds from Operations (FFO)*: FFO is a key metric for REITs, representing the cash generated from their core operations. Evaluate FFO to understand the REIT's ability to distribute dividends to shareholders.
- *Debt Levels and Interest Coverage*: Examine the REIT's debt levels and its ability to cover interest expenses. A manageable level of debt and sufficient interest coverage are crucial for financial stability.

5.4.3 Analyzing Management Teams and Track Records

The expertise and track record of a REIT's management team play a pivotal role in its success. Evaluate the qualifications and experience of key executives.

- *Management Expertise*: Assess the management team's expertise in real estate and their ability to navigate different market conditions. Look for a team with a proven track record in property acquisition, development, and management.

- *Alignment with Shareholders*: Consider whether the management team's interests align with those of shareholders. A management team with significant ownership in the REIT demonstrates a commitment to shareholder value.
- *Track Record in Value Creation*: Review the REIT's historical performance under the current management team. Assess their ability to create value through strategic decisions, property acquisitions, and portfolio management.

5.4.4 Utilizing Research Tools and Resources in REIT Selection

Investors have access to a variety of research tools and resources that can aid in the selection of REITs.

- *Financial News and Analysis*: Stay informed about financial news and analysis relevant to the real estate market and specific types of REITs. Financial news platforms and industry publications can provide valuable insights.
- *REIT-specific Research Reports*: Many financial institutions and research firms produce in-depth research reports on individual REITs or the real estate sector. These reports often include detailed analyses, forecasts, and recommendations.
- *Online Platforms and Screeners*: Utilize online platforms and screeners that allow you to filter and compare different REITs based on specific criteria. These tools can streamline the research process and help identify potential investment opportunities.

In conclusion, researching and selecting REITs require a multifaceted approach that encompasses fundamental analysis, financial statement evaluation, assessment of management teams, and the use of research tools and resources. Fundamental analysis involves understanding market conditions, evaluating property portfolios, and assessing key financial metrics. Reading financial statements helps gauge the REIT's financial health, and analyzing management teams ensures confidence in leadership. The use of research tools and resources, such as financial news platforms and online screeners, enhances the investor's ability to make well-informed decisions.

Chapter 6: Evaluating REITs

Section 1: Financial Metrics and Ratios

Evaluating Real Estate Investment Trusts (REITs) involves a comprehensive analysis of their financial health and performance metrics. In this section, we delve deeper into the key financial metrics and ratios used to assess REITs, including Funds from Operations (FFO), Adjusted Funds from Operations (AFFO), Net Operating Income (NOI), leverage and debt ratios, dividend payout ratios, and historical financial performance.

Analyzing the Financial Health of REITs

Assessing the financial health of REITs requires a thorough examination of various financial metrics and ratios that reflect their operational efficiency, profitability, and ability to generate cash flows.

6.1.1 Key Financial Metrics: FFO, AFFO, and NOI

- *Funds from Operations (FFO)*: FFO is a widely used metric for evaluating the operating performance of REITs. It represents the cash generated from a REIT's core operations and is calculated by adding depreciation and amortization expenses to earnings. FFO provides insight into the REIT's ability to generate cash flows from its properties.
- *Adjusted Funds from Operations (AFFO)*: AFFO adjusts FFO to account for recurring capital expenditures and other non-operating expenses necessary to maintain the REIT's properties. It provides a clearer picture of the cash available

for distribution to shareholders after accounting for essential property maintenance.

- *Net Operating Income (NOI)*: NOI is a measure of a property's operating income after deducting operating expenses but before deducting interest, depreciation, and amortization. It reflects the property's ability to generate rental income and is a key indicator of its profitability.

6.1.2 Understanding Leverage and Debt Ratios

Leverage and debt ratios provide insights into the REIT's capital structure and its ability to manage debt obligations responsibly.

- *Debt-to-Equity Ratio*: This ratio measures the proportion of debt financing relative to equity financing in the REIT's capital structure. A higher debt-to-equity ratio indicates higher financial leverage and may increase the REIT's risk exposure.
- *Interest Coverage Ratio*: The interest coverage ratio assesses the REIT's ability to meet its interest payment obligations. It compares the REIT's earnings before interest and taxes (EBIT) to its interest expenses. A higher interest coverage ratio indicates greater financial stability and ability to service debt.

6.1.3 Interpreting Dividend Payout Ratios

Dividend payout ratios indicate the proportion of earnings distributed to shareholders as dividends and help assess the sustainability of dividend payments.

- *Dividend Payout Ratio*: The dividend payout ratio measures the percentage of earnings distributed to shareholders as dividends. A lower dividend payout ratio indicates that the REIT retains more earnings for reinvestment or future distributions, while a higher ratio may suggest that the REIT is distributing a significant portion of its earnings.

6.1.4 Evaluating Historical Financial Performance

Analyzing the REIT's historical financial performance provides insights into its growth trajectory, profitability trends, and ability to weather economic cycles.

- *Revenue and Earnings Growth*: Assess the REIT's historical revenue and earnings growth rates over multiple periods. Consistent revenue and earnings growth indicate operational efficiency and management's ability to create value for shareholders.
- *Stability of Cash Flows*: Evaluate the stability and predictability of the REIT's cash flows over time. Consistent and predictable cash flows are essential for meeting debt obligations, funding property acquisitions, and distributing dividends to shareholders.

In conclusion, analyzing the financial health of REITs involves a multifaceted approach that considers key financial metrics and ratios, including FFO, AFFO, NOI, leverage and debt ratios, dividend payout ratios, and historical financial performance. These metrics provide valuable insights into the REIT's operational efficiency, profitability, leverage levels, dividend sustainability, and growth prospects. By conducting a comprehensive analysis of these factors, investors can make informed decisions and build a well-structured REIT portfolio aligned with their investment objectives and risk tolerance.

Section 2: Management Quality and Track Record

Assessing the quality of management is a critical aspect of evaluating Real Estate Investment Trusts (REITs). In this section, we explore the key factors to consider when evaluating the leadership and operational competence of a REIT, including the leadership team and their experience, corporate governance practices, historical performance of management, and communication and transparency.

Assessing Leadership and Operational Competence

The effectiveness of a REIT's management team directly influences its ability to navigate dynamic real estate markets, make strategic decisions, and create value for shareholders. Evaluating management quality involves a comprehensive analysis of both the leadership team and the operational practices they employ.

6.2.1 Leadership Team and Experience

- *Executive Leadership*: Begin by examining the backgrounds and qualifications of the executive leadership team. A seasoned team with diverse experiences in real estate, finance, and management is often an indicator of a well-rounded and capable leadership.
- *Industry Expertise*: Assess the team's expertise within the real estate industry. Experience in property acquisition, development, and management is crucial for effectively navigating the challenges and opportunities within the market.
- *Relevant Track Record*: Look for a track record of success in managing similar types of properties or real estate portfolios.

The ability to demonstrate successful execution in the past enhances confidence in the team's capabilities.

6.2.2 Corporate Governance Practices

Corporate governance plays a vital role in ensuring transparency, accountability, and ethical behavior within a REIT. Investors should evaluate the REIT's governance practices to ensure alignment with shareholder interests.

- *Board Independence*: A board of directors with a sufficient level of independence is essential for effective oversight. An independent board helps mitigate conflicts of interest and ensures decisions are made in the best interests of shareholders.
- *Executive Compensation*: Evaluate the alignment of executive compensation with the REIT's performance and shareholder value creation. A transparent and performance-based compensation structure is indicative of a commitment to aligning management interests with shareholders.
- *Shareholder Rights*: Consider the rights afforded to shareholders, such as voting rights and access to information. Robust shareholder rights contribute to a more democratic and accountable governance structure.

6.2.3 Historical Performance of Management

Examining the historical performance of a REIT's management provides valuable insights into their ability to navigate different market conditions and create value for shareholders.

- *Property Acquisition and Disposition*: Evaluate the success of past property acquisitions and dispositions. Assess whether the management team has demonstrated a strategic and disciplined approach to optimizing the REIT's property portfolio.

- *Financial Performance*: Analyze the historical financial performance of the REIT under the current management team. Look for consistent growth in key financial metrics such as FFO, NOI, and dividends per share.
- *Execution of Strategic Initiatives*: Assess the execution of strategic initiatives outlined by the management team. Successful execution of business plans and strategic goals indicates effective leadership.

6.2.4 Communication and Transparency

Effective communication and transparency are crucial for maintaining trust and keeping shareholders well-informed. Evaluate the REIT's practices in communicating with investors and disclosing relevant information.

- *Investor Relations Practices*: Assess the quality of the REIT's investor relations practices, including the availability of timely financial reports, earnings calls, and other communications. Transparent communication enhances investor confidence.
- *Risk Disclosure*: Look for thorough and transparent disclosure of risks associated with the REIT's operations. A transparent approach to risk disclosure demonstrates a commitment to providing investors with a comprehensive understanding of potential challenges.
- *Accessibility to Management*: Consider whether the management team is accessible to shareholders and responsive

to inquiries. Open lines of communication indicate a commitment to engaging with and addressing the concerns of investors.

In conclusion, assessing the quality of management is a crucial step in evaluating REITs. A strong leadership team with relevant experience, effective corporate governance practices, a positive historical performance record, and transparent communication contribute to the overall strength and credibility of a REIT. Investors should conduct thorough due diligence on these factors to make informed investment decisions aligned with their financial goals and risk tolerance.

Section 3: Property Portfolio Analysis

Scrutinizing the composition of a Real Estate Investment Trust's (REIT) property holdings is a fundamental aspect of the evaluation process. In this section, we delve into the key factors involved in property portfolio analysis, including property types and locations, tenant diversity and lease terms, the age and condition of properties, and assessing portfolio growth strategies.

Scrutinizing the Composition of REIT Property Holdings

The composition of a REIT's property portfolio is a critical determinant of its overall performance and resilience in the face of market fluctuations. A thorough analysis of various aspects of the property portfolio provides investors with insights into the REIT's risk profile, income stability, and potential for future growth.

6.3.1 Property Types and Locations

- *Diversification Across Property Types*: Evaluate the diversification of the REIT's property holdings across different types such as residential, commercial, retail, healthcare, and infrastructure. Diversification helps mitigate risks associated with the performance of a specific property type.

- *Geographical Distribution*: Assess the geographical distribution of the properties. A well-diversified portfolio with properties in different regions or markets may be more resilient to localized economic downturns or market-specific challenges.
- *Strategic Focus*: Understand the REIT's strategic focus in terms of property types and locations. A clear and well-defined strategy indicates a thoughtful approach to portfolio construction and management.

6.3.2 Tenant Diversity and Lease Terms

- *Tenant Mix*: Analyze the diversity of tenants within the portfolio. A well-diversified tenant mix reduces the risk associated with dependence on a small number of tenants. Consider the types of businesses represented and their respective industries.
- *Lease Expirations and Terms*: Evaluate the lease expiration schedule and terms. A staggered lease expiration schedule can contribute to income stability, as it prevents a significant portion of leases from expiring simultaneously. Additionally, favorable lease terms, such as long-term leases with rent escalations, enhance predictability.
- *Tenant Credit Quality*: Consider the credit quality of the tenants. Strong and creditworthy tenants contribute to stable rental income, while a concentration of tenants with weaker credit may pose higher risks.

6.3.3 Age and Condition of Properties

- *Property Age*: Assess the age distribution of the properties within the portfolio. While older properties may have historical charm, newer properties often require less maintenance and may offer modern amenities that appeal to tenants.
- *Maintenance and Upkeep*: Consider the condition of the properties and the REIT's commitment to maintenance and improvements. Regular maintenance and strategic upgrades contribute to the longevity and attractiveness of the properties.
- *Capital Expenditure Planning*: Evaluate the REIT's capital expenditure planning for property improvements and renovations. A proactive approach to maintaining and enhancing property value demonstrates a commitment to long-term value creation.

6.3.4 Assessing Portfolio Growth Strategies

- *Acquisition and Disposition History*: Examine the REIT's historical record of property acquisitions and dispositions. Assess the strategic rationale behind these transactions and their impact on the overall portfolio. Consistent and strategic growth initiatives indicate effective management.
- *Development and Expansion Plans*: Understand the REIT's plans for property development and expansion. A clear strategy for developing new properties or expanding existing ones reflects a proactive approach to portfolio growth and responding to market opportunities.
- *Risk Mitigation Strategies*: Evaluate the REIT's strategies for

mitigating risks within the property portfolio. This may include measures to address market-specific challenges, economic downturns, or shifts in tenant demand.

In conclusion, scrutinizing the composition of a REIT's property holdings is a crucial step in evaluating its potential for long-term success. Property portfolio analysis involves assessing the diversification across property types and locations, evaluating tenant diversity and lease terms, considering the age and condition of properties, and examining the effectiveness of portfolio growth strategies. By conducting a thorough analysis of these factors, investors can gain a comprehensive understanding of the REIT's risk profile, income stability, and growth potential.

Section 4: Market and Economic Conditions

Considering external factors affecting Real Estate Investment Trust (REIT) performance is crucial for making informed investment decisions. In this section, we explore the impact of interest rates on REITs, macro-economic trends and real estate market conditions, regulatory and legislative developments, and global and regional economic influences.

Considering External Factors Affecting REIT Performance

REITs operate within dynamic environments shaped by various external factors. Investors must evaluate these factors to gauge a REIT's resilience, adaptability, and potential for long-term success.

6.4.1 Impact of Interest Rates on REITs

- *Interest Rate Sensitivity*: Understand how changes in interest rates can affect REIT performance. In a rising interest rate environment, REITs may face higher financing costs, potentially impacting their profitability. Conversely, falling interest rates can enhance the attractiveness of REITs for income-seeking investors.

- *Interest Rate Risk Management*: Assess the REIT's strategies for managing interest rate risks. This may involve using fixed-rate debt, interest rate hedges, or other financial instruments to mitigate the impact of interest rate fluctuations.

6.4.2 Macro-Economic Trends and Real Estate Market Conditions

- *Economic Indicators*: Evaluate the REIT's sensitivity to macro-economic trends. Economic indicators such as GDP growth, employment rates, and consumer spending can influence demand for different types of real estate and impact the overall performance of a REIT.
- *Real Estate Market Conditions*: Analyze the current conditions of the real estate market in which the REIT operates. Consider factors such as vacancy rates, rental growth, and property values to assess the overall health of the market and the potential for the REIT to capitalize on market opportunities.

6.4.3 Regulatory and Legislative Developments

- *Legal and Regulatory Framework*: Examine the legal and regulatory environment in which the REIT operates. Changes in regulations related to real estate, taxation, or financial markets can significantly impact REIT performance. Assess the REIT's ability to adapt to regulatory changes and its proactive approach to compliance.

- *Legislative Impact on Property Types*: Understand how legislative developments may affect specific property types within the REIT's portfolio. For example, changes in healthcare regulations may impact healthcare REITs, while alterations in zoning laws can affect commercial or residential properties.

6.4.4 Global and Regional Economic Influences on REITs

- *Global Economic Factors*: Consider the influence of global economic trends on REIT performance. Factors such as trade policies, geopolitical events, and global economic downturns can have ripple effects on real estate markets and, consequently, on REITs.
- *Regional Economic Variances*: Assess how regional economic variations may affect different segments of the REIT's portfolio. Diversification across regions can help mitigate risks associated with regional economic downturns or uncertainties.

Understanding and monitoring these external factors require ongoing diligence and adaptability. Successful REIT investment involves anticipating and responding to changes in market and economic conditions.

In conclusion, evaluating REITs goes beyond assessing internal factors and financial metrics; it necessitates a comprehensive understanding of the external factors influencing their performance. The impact of interest rates, macro-economic trends, regulatory developments, and global and regional economic influences collectively shapes the landscape in which REITs operate. Investors who integrate this holistic perspective into their analysis are better equipped to make well-informed decisions aligned with their investment goals and risk tolerance.

Chapter 7: Creating a Passive Income Stream

Section 1: Dividend Yields and Distribution Frequency

Generating a passive income stream is a primary goal for many investors, and Real Estate Investment Trusts (REITs) offer a compelling avenue for achieving this objective. In this section, we explore the fundamentals of REIT dividend distributions, including calculating dividend yields, understanding the impact of distribution frequency on income, and assessing the historical dividend performance of REITs.

Understanding the Basics of REIT Dividend Distributions

REITs are renowned for their consistent dividend distributions, making them an attractive option for income-focused investors. Understanding the basics of how these dividends are structured and distributed is key to creating a reliable passive income stream.

7.1.1 Calculating Dividend Yields

- *Dividend Yield Formula*: The dividend yield is a crucial metric for income investors, representing the annual dividend income relative to the investment's price. The formula is expressed as follows:

Dividend Yield = (Annual Dividends per Share / Current Share Price) × 100

- *Interpreting Dividend Yields*: A higher dividend yield is generally desirable, indicating a higher income potential relative to the investment. However, investors should balance this with other factors, such as the sustainability of dividends and the overall health of the REIT.

7.1.2 Impact of Distribution Frequency on Income

- *Monthly vs. Quarterly Distributions*: REITs may distribute dividends on a monthly or quarterly basis. Monthly distributions provide a more frequent income stream, while quarterly distributions might be associated with higher dividend yields. Understanding the investor's cash flow needs and preferences is crucial in choosing between these distribution frequencies.
- *Tax Implications*: Different distribution frequencies may have varying tax implications for investors. It's essential to consider how the timing and frequency of dividends align with personal tax planning strategies.

7.1.3 Historical Dividend Performance of REITs

- *Consistency and Growth*: Analyzing the historical dividend performance of a REIT provides insights into its ability to generate a reliable income stream. Consistent or growing dividends over time indicate a financially healthy and well-managed REIT.
- *Payout Ratios*: Evaluate the REIT's payout ratios, comparing the amount of earnings allocated to dividends. Sustainable dividend growth is often associated with payout ratios that leave room for future investment, property development, and market fluctuations.

Creating a passive income stream through REIT investments requires a strategic approach to assessing dividend-related factors. Investors should aim for a balance between high dividend yields, sustainable distribution frequencies, and a history of reliable and growing dividend payments.

Section 2: Reinvesting Dividends vs. Cash Payouts

Managing dividend income is a pivotal aspect of creating a passive income stream through Real Estate Investment Trusts (REITs). In this section, we explore the options available for investors in handling their dividend income, including the advantages and disadvantages of dividend reinvestment programs, building wealth through dividend reinvestment, and the alternative choice of opting for cash payouts for liquidity.

Exploring Options for Managing Dividend Income

REIT investors often face a crucial decision regarding what to do with their received dividends. Understanding the available options and their implications is essential for aligning investment strategies with financial goals.

7.2.1 Advantages and Disadvantages of Reinvestment Programs

- *Advantages of Dividend Reinvestment*: Participating in dividend reinvestment programs (DRIPs) can offer several advantages. By automatically reinvesting dividends back into additional shares of the REIT, investors can benefit from compounding returns over time. This process harnesses the power of time and capital appreciation, potentially leading to accelerated wealth accumulation.

- *Compounding Returns*: The compounding effect results from earning returns not just on the original investment but also on the reinvested dividends. Over an extended period, this compounding can significantly enhance the overall return on investment.
- *Cost Averaging*: DRIPs typically allow investors to purchase additional shares at the market price, often at a discount. This practice of dollar-cost averaging can help smooth out the impact of market volatility.
- *Disadvantages of Dividend Reinvestment*: While DRIPs offer compelling advantages, investors should be aware of potential drawbacks. Reinvesting dividends may lead to overconcentration in a particular asset, especially if the REIT's performance is volatile. Additionally, the automatic nature of DRIPs may limit an investor's ability to deploy funds strategically in other investment opportunities.

7.2.2 Building Wealth through Dividend Reinvestment

- *Long-Term Wealth Building*: The primary goal of reinvesting dividends is to build long-term wealth. This strategy aligns with a buy-and-hold approach, leveraging the power of compounding returns over an extended period.
- *Retirement Planning*: Dividend reinvestment can be particularly advantageous for investors planning for retirement. Over time, the growing number of shares through reinvestment can contribute to a more substantial income stream during retirement.
- *Tax Considerations*: Investors should consider the tax implications of dividend reinvestment. While dividends reinvested are not immediately taxed, the capital gains

realized upon eventual sale may have tax implications. Investors should consult with tax professionals to understand the specific tax consequences in their jurisdiction.

7.2.3 Opting for Cash Payouts and Liquidity

- *Immediate Income and Flexibility*: Opting for cash payouts provides investors with immediate income, offering flexibility in how they deploy these funds. This liquidity can be valuable for addressing short-term financial needs, taking advantage of other investment opportunities, or maintaining a cash reserve for emergencies.
- *Income Diversification*: Cash payouts allow investors to diversify their income sources. By having the flexibility to allocate dividends elsewhere, investors can create a more balanced and diversified income portfolio.
- *Market Timing Opportunities*: Having cash on hand provides investors with the opportunity to time their investments strategically. This can be particularly advantageous during periods of market volatility or when specific investment opportunities arise.

In conclusion, the choice between reinvesting dividends and opting for cash payouts involves weighing the advantages and disadvantages of each strategy based on individual financial goals, risk tolerance, and investment horizon. For long-term wealth building and retirement planning, dividend reinvestment can be a powerful strategy, harnessing the benefits of compounding returns. On the other hand, choosing cash payouts offers immediate income and the flexibility to adapt to changing financial circumstances or capitalize on market opportunities. As investors navigate this decision, they should align their chosen strategy with their broader financial plan and regularly reassess it based on evolving goals and market conditions.

Section 3: Strategies for Maximizing Passive Income

Maximizing passive income through Real Estate Investment Trusts (REITs) requires a strategic approach that goes beyond the basics of dividend distributions. In this section, we explore tactics to enhance REIT income generation, including diversifying across high-yielding REITs, identifying REITs with consistent dividend growth, timing and strategies for income maximization, and balancing income goals with risk tolerance.

Implementing Tactics to Enhance REIT Income Generation

While passive income is a key attraction of REIT investing, implementing specific strategies can amplify its impact. Investors seeking to maximize their income should consider a nuanced approach that aligns with their financial objectives and risk appetite.

7.3.1 Diversifying Across High-Yielding REITs

- *Diversification Benefits*: Diversifying across different REITs, especially those with varying property types and geographical locations, can enhance income stability. High-yielding REITs may belong to different sectors, such as commercial, residential, or healthcare, providing a balanced approach to income generation.
- *Risk Mitigation*: While high-yielding REITs can offer attractive income potential, investors should balance this with a consideration of risk. Diversification helps spread risk across

various assets, reducing the impact of underperformance in any single investment.

- *Sector Analysis*: Conduct thorough research into different sectors to identify high-yielding REITs. Consider market trends, demand dynamics, and economic factors that may influence the performance of specific sectors.

7.3.2 Identifying REITs with Consistent Dividend Growth

- *Dividend Growth as a Metric*: Beyond current dividend yields, investors should evaluate the historical performance of REITs in terms of dividend growth. REITs with a track record of consistent dividend increases may indicate financial health and effective management.
- *Evaluating Payout Ratios*: Assess the REIT's payout ratios to ensure that dividend growth is sustainable. A lower payout ratio suggests that the REIT retains a significant portion of earnings for potential future growth and stability.
- *Long-Term Income Growth*: Investing in REITs with consistent dividend growth aligns with a strategy of long-term income growth. This approach can be particularly appealing for investors with a focus on building a resilient and steadily increasing passive income stream.

7.3.3 Timing and Strategies for Income Maximization

- *Market Timing*: Consider market timing strategies to optimize income generation. For example, investors might strategically reinvest dividends during periods of lower market valuations or allocate funds to high-yielding REITs when their prices are temporarily suppressed.

- *Utilizing Dividend Reinvestment Plans (DRIPs)*: DRIPs can be utilized strategically to reinvest dividends at opportune times. Investors may choose to reinvest dividends when market conditions are favorable or when specific REITs offer discounted prices.
- *Systematic Investment*: Implementing a systematic investment approach, such as dollar-cost averaging, can be effective in optimizing income maximization. This involves regularly investing a fixed amount, which can lead to purchasing more shares when prices are lower and fewer shares when prices are higher.

7.3.4 Balancing Income Goals with Risk Tolerance

- *Risk Assessment*: Align income goals with an assessment of risk tolerance. While higher-yielding REITs may offer attractive income potential, they often come with elevated risk. Investors should carefully evaluate their risk tolerance and consider a balanced approach that meets income objectives while managing risk.
- *Portfolio Rebalancing*: Regularly reassess and rebalance the REIT portfolio to align with evolving income goals and risk tolerance. Adjustments may be necessary based on changes in market conditions, economic outlook, or individual financial circumstances.
- *Understanding Volatility*: Acknowledge that higher-yielding investments may be more susceptible to volatility. Understanding the potential for price fluctuations and incorporating this into risk management strategies is crucial for maintaining a stable income stream.

In conclusion, maximizing passive income through REITs involves a thoughtful combination of diversification, identifying consistent dividend growth, strategic timing, and aligning income goals with risk tolerance. By implementing these tactics, investors can tailor their REIT portfolio to generate a reliable and growing passive income stream.

Chapter 8: Tax Considerations for REIT Investors

Section 1: Taxation of REIT Dividends

Understanding the tax treatment of Real Estate Investment Trust (REIT) dividends is crucial for investors to make informed decisions and optimize their overall tax strategy. In this section, we delve into the taxation of REIT dividend income, including differentiating ordinary income and qualified dividends, taxation rates on REIT dividends, and the impact of the holding period on taxation.

Understanding the Tax Treatment of REIT Dividend Income

Investors in REITs benefit from the pass-through nature of these entities, which allows income to flow directly to shareholders. However, the tax treatment of REIT dividends involves various nuances that investors should consider.

8.1.1 Differentiating Ordinary Income and Qualified Dividends

- *Ordinary Income*: The majority of REIT dividends are treated as ordinary income. Unlike qualified dividends, which benefit from lower tax rates, ordinary income is subject to an investor's regular income tax rates. Investors should be aware of their income tax brackets to understand the potential tax liability associated with their REIT dividends.
- *Qualified Dividends*: While REIT dividends are typically considered ordinary income, some portions may qualify as

qualified dividends. To be considered qualified, specific criteria must be met, including the REIT meeting holding period requirements. Qualified dividends are subject to lower tax rates, similar to long-term capital gains.

8.1.2 Taxation Rates on REIT Dividends

- *Ordinary Income Tax Rates*: As ordinary income, most REIT dividends are taxed at an investor's regular income tax rates. These rates vary depending on an individual's income bracket, with higher-income individuals facing higher tax rates.
- *Qualified Dividend Tax Rates*: If certain criteria are met, a portion of REIT dividends may qualify for lower tax rates. For the tax year 2022, the maximum tax rate on qualified dividends is 20% for individuals in the highest income tax bracket, while those in lower brackets may benefit from even lower rates, including 0% for some.

8.1.3 Impact of Holding Period on Taxation

- *Holding Period for Qualified Dividends*: To qualify for the lower tax rates applicable to qualified dividends, investors must meet specific holding period requirements. Typically, the investor must hold the REIT shares for more than 60 days during the 121-day period that begins 60 days before the ex-dividend date. This holding period requirement is designed to encourage long-term investment.
- *Short-Term Capital Gains*: If the holding period requirement for qualified dividends is not met, the dividends may be treated as short-term capital gains and taxed at the investor's ordinary income tax rates. It's crucial for investors to track

their holding periods to ensure they meet the criteria for favorable tax treatment.

Understanding the tax treatment of REIT dividends allows investors to develop tax-efficient strategies aligned with their financial goals. While most REIT dividends are taxed as ordinary income, the potential for qualified dividends introduces an opportunity for lower tax rates. Investors should carefully monitor their holding periods and consider tax-efficient strategies to optimize their after-tax returns.

Section 2: Avoiding the Double Taxation Trap

Minimizing tax liabilities is a fundamental goal for investors in Real Estate Investment Trusts (REITs). In this section, we explore strategies to avoid the double taxation trap associated with certain investment structures. This includes recognizing the potential for double taxation, utilizing tax credits and deductions, and choosing tax-efficient investment vehicles.

Exploring Strategies to Minimize Tax Liabilities

Understanding the potential for double taxation and employing effective strategies is crucial for investors aiming to optimize their after-tax returns.

8.2.1 Recognizing the Potential for Double Taxation

- *Corporate Taxation*: Traditional corporations are subject to corporate income tax on their profits. If a company distributes dividends to its shareholders, those dividends are then taxed as income at the individual level. This results in double taxation — once at the corporate level and again at the individual level.
- *Pass-Through Nature of REITs*: REITs, on the other hand, are

structured as pass-through entities. They do not pay corporate income tax on their earnings. Instead, income is passed through to investors, who are responsible for paying taxes on their share of the income. This pass-through structure helps avoid the double taxation trap associated with traditional corporations.

8.2.2 Utilizing Tax Credits and Deductions

- *Tax Credits*: Investors should explore available tax credits to offset their overall tax liabilities. While tax credits directly reduce the amount of taxes owed, they may be subject to specific eligibility criteria. Some tax credits are designed to encourage investment in certain sectors or activities and may apply to REIT investments.
- *Deductions for Investment Expenses*: Investors can potentially deduct certain investment-related expenses, such as advisory fees and expenses directly associated with the production of income. Proper record-keeping and consultation with tax professionals are crucial to ensure eligibility for deductions.

8.2.3 Choosing Tax-Efficient Investment Vehicles

- *Tax-Efficient Structures*: Beyond REITs, investors can explore other tax-efficient investment structures. For example, exchange-traded funds (ETFs) that focus on real estate may offer tax advantages. ETFs are designed to minimize capital gains distributions, providing tax efficiency for investors.
- *Individual Retirement Accounts (IRAs)*: Investing in REITs through tax-advantaged accounts, such as IRAs, can contribute to overall tax efficiency. Earnings within IRAs

grow tax-deferred, and qualified withdrawals may be taxed at lower rates.

- *Tax-Managed Funds*: Consider tax-managed funds that prioritize tax efficiency in their investment strategies. These funds aim to minimize taxable distributions, making them suitable for investors seeking to reduce their tax burdens.

By recognizing the potential for double taxation and implementing strategies to mitigate tax liabilities, investors can enhance the overall tax efficiency of their investment portfolios. Utilizing available tax credits, exploring deductions, and choosing tax-efficient investment vehicles contribute to a comprehensive approach to minimize tax burdens.

Section 3: Tax-Efficient Strategies for REIT Investors

As investors navigate the complex landscape of Real Estate Investment Trust (REIT) investments, optimizing tax efficiency becomes paramount. In this section, we explore tax-efficient strategies for REIT investors, including asset location and tax-loss harvesting, utilizing tax-advantaged accounts, timing strategies for tax planning, and the importance of collaborating with tax professionals for guidance.

Implementing Techniques to Optimize Tax Efficiency

Maximizing after-tax returns requires a thoughtful approach to tax planning. By implementing specific techniques, investors can enhance tax efficiency and potentially reduce their overall tax burden.

8.3.1 Asset Location and Tax-Loss Harvesting

- *Asset Location Strategies*: Strategic placement of assets across different types of accounts can contribute to tax efficiency. Considerations include placing tax-inefficient investments in tax-advantaged accounts, such as Individual Retirement Accounts (IRAs), while holding tax-efficient investments in taxable accounts.

- *Tax-Loss Harvesting*: Actively managing investment portfolios through tax-loss harvesting involves selling investments with losses to offset gains, thereby reducing the overall tax liability. Investors can strategically leverage losses within their REIT portfolio to offset capital gains and potentially generate tax savings.

8.3.2 Tax-Advantaged Accounts for REIT Investments

- *Individual Retirement Accounts (IRAs)*: Investing in REITs through IRAs provides tax advantages. Earnings within IRAs grow tax-deferred, allowing investors to postpone taxes until withdrawals are made. Traditional IRAs offer tax deductions on contributions, while Roth IRAs may provide tax-free withdrawals in retirement.
- *Health Savings Accounts (HSAs)*: For eligible individuals with High Deductible Health Plans (HDHPs), Health Savings Accounts can offer triple tax benefits. Contributions are tax-deductible, earnings grow tax-free, and withdrawals for qualified medical expenses are also tax-free. While primarily designed for healthcare expenses, HSAs can be used as a tax-efficient investment vehicle.

8.3.3 Timing Strategies for Tax Planning

- *Tax-Loss Harvesting Timing*: Understanding the tax

implications of the timing of investment actions is crucial. Tax-loss harvesting should be executed strategically, considering individual tax situations, market conditions, and the potential for offsetting gains.

- *Strategic Withdrawals from Tax-Advantaged Accounts*: In retirement, careful planning of withdrawals from tax-advantaged accounts can optimize tax efficiency. By managing the timing and amount of withdrawals, investors can minimize tax liability and potentially extend the longevity of their portfolios.

8.3.4 Working with Tax Professionals for Guidance

- *Customized Tax Planning Strategies*: Every investor's tax situation is unique, influenced by factors such as income level, filing status, and investment portfolio composition. Collaborating with tax professionals, including Certified Public Accountants (CPAs) or tax advisors, ensures the development of customized tax planning strategies aligned with individual financial goals.
- *Staying Informed about Tax Law Changes*: Tax laws can undergo changes, impacting the treatment of investment income, deductions, and credits. Tax professionals stay abreast of these changes and provide guidance on how investors can adapt their strategies to remain tax-efficient.
- *Comprehensive Financial Planning*: Tax professionals can integrate tax planning into a broader financial planning framework. This includes aligning investment strategies with overall financial goals, estate planning considerations, and retirement planning. A holistic approach ensures that tax efficiency is a central component of the overall financial

strategy.

In conclusion, implementing tax-efficient strategies for REIT investments requires a nuanced understanding of asset location, tax-loss harvesting, the utilization of tax-advantaged accounts, timing considerations, and collaboration with tax professionals. Investors should actively engage in tax planning as an integral part of their overall investment strategy to optimize after-tax returns.

Section 4: Estate Planning and Gift Tax Considerations

As investors build and manage their Real Estate Investment Trust (REIT) portfolios, it is essential to address long-term wealth transfer strategies through effective estate planning. In this section, we delve into estate tax implications for REIT investors, gifting strategies to reduce tax exposure, incorporating REITs into comprehensive estate plans, and staying informed about changes in tax legislation.

Addressing Long-Term Wealth Transfer Strategies

Estate planning is a critical aspect of financial management, particularly for individuals seeking to pass on their wealth to future generations. As REITs play a role in many investment portfolios, understanding the implications of estate taxes and implementing strategic gifting strategies are crucial components of long-term wealth transfer planning.

8.4.1 Estate Tax Implications for REIT Investors

- *Estate Tax Basics*: The federal estate tax is levied on the transfer of a person's estate upon their death. As of the knowledge cutoff in January 2022, estates valued above a certain threshold (the exemption amount) are subject to estate taxes. The exemption amount is subject to change due to updates in tax laws.

- *Inclusion of REITs in the Estate*: When an individual holds REIT investments, the value of these holdings is considered part of their estate for estate tax purposes. As the estate tax is determined based on the total value of the estate, including real estate assets like REITs, it is essential for investors to be aware of potential estate tax implications.

8.4.2 Gifting Strategies to Reduce Tax Exposure

- *Annual Gift Tax Exclusion*: Individuals can make gifts of a certain amount each year to others without triggering gift taxes. Leveraging the annual gift tax exclusion allows for the gradual transfer of wealth without impacting the lifetime exemption. This strategy is particularly useful for reducing the taxable value of the estate.
- *Lifetime Gift Tax Exemption*: In addition to the annual gift tax exclusion, individuals have a lifetime gift tax exemption, which allows for more significant transfers without incurring immediate taxes. Gifting strategies involving REITs can be designed to take advantage of this exemption while aligning with overall estate planning goals.

8.4.3 Incorporating REITs into Comprehensive Estate Plans

- *Family Limited Partnerships (FLPs) and Limited Liability Companies (LLCs)*: Creating FLPs or LLCs can provide a structured way to transfer REIT holdings to heirs. By consolidating ownership and maintaining control, families can strategically manage the transfer of REIT assets while potentially reducing estate taxes.

- *Irrevocable Trusts*: Establishing irrevocable trusts can be an effective means of transferring REIT assets while providing specific guidelines for distribution. Irrevocable trusts remove assets from the taxable estate, offering potential tax advantages.
- *Charitable Remainder Trusts (CRTs)*: CRTs allow individuals to donate assets, including REITs, to a charitable trust while retaining income from the assets during their lifetime. This strategy provides both charitable benefits and potential estate tax advantages.

8.4.4 Staying Informed about Changes in Tax Legislation

- *Dynamic Nature of Tax Laws*: Tax laws are subject to change, and staying informed about updates is crucial for effective estate planning. Changes in exemption amounts, rates, and other provisions can impact the strategies employed by investors. Regular consultations with tax professionals help ensure that estate plans remain aligned with current tax legislation.
- *Flexibility in Planning*: Recognizing the potential for changes in tax laws, it's important to build flexibility into estate plans. This allows for adjustments to be made in response to new legislative developments, ensuring that plans remain effective and compliant with the latest regulations.

Additionally, the integration of REITs into comprehensive estate plans requires careful consideration and collaboration with estate planning professionals to create a tailored strategy that aligns with an investor's specific goals and circumstances.

Chapter 9: Monitoring and Adjusting Your REIT Portfolio

Section 1: Regular Portfolio Review

Investing in Real Estate Investment Trusts (REITs) requires a disciplined and strategic approach. A crucial aspect of this approach is establishing a routine for comprehensive portfolio assessment. This section delves into the importance of regular check-ins, setting a schedule for portfolio reviews, identifying key metrics and indicators for evaluation, and leveraging technology for effective portfolio tracking.

9.1.1 Importance of Regular Check-ins

Continuous Performance Monitoring: Regular portfolio reviews are essential for investors to monitor the ongoing performance of their REIT investments. The real estate market, influenced by various economic factors, undergoes dynamic changes, and a regular check-in ensures that investors stay informed about their portfolio's health.

Adaptation to Market Conditions: The financial landscape can shift rapidly, impacting the performance of REITs. Regular check-ins enable investors to adapt their strategies to changing market conditions. Whether responding to economic trends, interest rate fluctuations, or shifts in consumer behavior, staying vigilant allows for timely adjustments to the portfolio.

Opportunity Identification: Markets present new opportunities and challenges regularly. By conducting regular reviews, investors can identify emerging trends or sectors showing potential for growth. This proactive approach empowers investors to capitalize on opportunities and reallocate resources accordingly.

Risk Mitigation: Regular assessments help in identifying and mitigating risks promptly. Investors can evaluate the impact of market changes on their portfolio and take measures to reduce risk exposure. This could involve diversification, adjusting asset allocation, or revising investment goals to align with current market conditions.

9.1.2 Setting a Schedule for Portfolio Reviews

Frequency of Reviews: The frequency of portfolio reviews depends on various factors, including an investor's risk tolerance, investment horizon, and market conditions. While some investors may prefer quarterly reviews, others may opt for more frequent assessments. A common approach is to conduct a comprehensive review at least annually, with interim checks as needed.

Aligning with Financial Goals: The schedule for portfolio reviews should align with an investor's financial goals and the nature of their investments. For those with a long-term investment horizon, less frequent reviews may be suitable, while short-term investors may benefit from more regular assessments.

Event-Driven Reviews: In addition to scheduled reviews, investors should consider event-driven assessments. Major economic events, changes in interest rates, or shifts in legislation can warrant unscheduled reviews to ensure the portfolio remains resilient in the face of unexpected developments.

9.1.3 Metrics and Indicators to Evaluate

Performance Metrics: Assessing the performance of REIT investments involves examining key metrics. These may include total return, dividend yield, and funds from operations (FFO). Analyzing historical performance against benchmarks provides insights into how well the portfolio is meeting its financial objectives.

Diversification Metrics: Diversification is a cornerstone of risk management. Investors should evaluate the diversity of their REIT portfolio across property types, geographical regions, and market sectors. This helps ensure that the portfolio is not overly concentrated in a specific area, mitigating risks associated with a single market's performance.

Risk-Adjusted Returns: Evaluating risk-adjusted returns is crucial for understanding the efficiency of the portfolio. Metrics such as the Sharpe ratio can provide insights into how well the portfolio generates returns relative to its level of risk. Investors aiming for optimal risk-adjusted returns can use these metrics to fine-tune their investment strategy.

Income Generation Metrics: For investors seeking income generation, metrics related to dividend performance are vital. Dividend yield, payout ratios, and consistency of dividend payments are key indicators. Regularly assessing these metrics ensures that the portfolio aligns with income-oriented investment goals.

9.1.4 Utilizing Technology for Portfolio Tracking

Portfolio Management Tools: Technology plays a pivotal role in modern portfolio management. Numerous online platforms and tools provide investors with the capability to track and manage their REIT portfolios effectively. These tools often offer real-time updates, performance analytics, and customizable dashboards for a holistic view of the portfolio.

Automated Alerts: Setting up automated alerts for significant events or changes in the market can keep investors informed in real-time. This proactive approach allows for timely decision-making and ensures that investors are not caught off guard by sudden market developments.

Digital Analytics and Data Visualization: Technology facilitates data-driven decision-making through advanced analytics and data visualization. Investors can leverage these tools to gain deeper insights into their portfolio's performance, identify patterns, and make informed decisions based on historical and real-time data.

Mobile Accessibility: In the era of mobile technology, investors can track their portfolios on the go. Mobile apps and platforms enable investors to access their portfolio information, receive alerts, and execute trades from their smartphones, providing convenience and flexibility.

Conclusion

Establishing a routine for regular portfolio review is an integral part of successful REIT investing. Through consistent check-ins, investors can adapt to market dynamics, identify opportunities, and mitigate risks. Setting a schedule aligned with financial goals, evaluating key metrics, and leveraging technology for effective tracking ensures that the portfolio remains optimized for long-term success. Regular assessments empower investors

Section 2: Responding to Market Changes

Effective investment management involves not only regular reviews but also the ability to respond to dynamic market conditions. In this section, we explore the strategies for adapting to market changes, identifying trends and shifts, evaluating the impact of economic events on Real Estate Investment Trusts (REITs), understanding market sentiment, and implementing strategies to navigate both bull and bear markets.

Adapting to Dynamic Market Conditions

Investing in REITs requires a dynamic approach, especially considering the ever-changing nature of financial markets. Reacting effectively to market changes is a skill that can contribute significantly to the success of a REIT portfolio.

9.2.1 Identifying Market Trends and Shifts

- *Technical Analysis*: Utilizing technical analysis tools and charts can help investors identify trends and potential shifts in the market. Analyzing historical price movements, trading volumes, and key technical indicators can provide insights into the direction of the market.
- *Fundamental Analysis*: Examining the underlying factors affecting the real estate market and specific sectors within REITs is crucial for understanding broader trends. Economic indicators, interest rates, and demographic shifts are among the fundamental factors influencing market trends.

9.2.2 Evaluating the Impact of Economic Events on REITs

- *Interest Rate Movements*: Changes in interest rates can significantly impact the performance of REITs. Rising interest rates may lead to higher borrowing costs and reduced property valuations, affecting the overall profitability of

REITs. Conversely, falling interest rates may create favorable conditions for REITs.

- *Economic Indicators*: Monitoring economic indicators, such as GDP growth, employment rates, and consumer spending, provides insights into the overall health of the economy. Economic events, such as recessions or expansions, can have varying effects on different types of REITs.

9.2.3 Market Sentiment and Its Influence on Decision-Making

- *Contrarian Investing*: Understanding market sentiment involves recognizing when the market may be overly optimistic or pessimistic. Contrarian investors may consider going against prevailing sentiment, buying when others are selling in a bear market or selling when others are overly optimistic in a bull market.
- *Behavioral Finance Considerations*: Behavioral biases can influence market sentiment and decision-making. Recognizing common biases, such as herd mentality and fear of missing out (FOMO), allows investors to make more informed and rational decisions.

9.2.4 Strategies for Navigating Bull and Bear Markets

- *Bull Markets*: In bullish conditions, investors may focus on growth-oriented strategies. This could involve increasing exposure to REITs with potential for capital appreciation, while remaining vigilant for signs of potential market overheating.
- *Bear Markets*: During bear markets, preserving capital becomes a priority. Defensive strategies may include reducing

exposure to more volatile REITs, increasing allocations to defensive sectors, and considering alternative investments with lower correlation to traditional markets.

Adapting to dynamic market conditions requires a combination of analytical skills, market awareness, and a disciplined approach to decision-making. Investors in REITs should be proactive in staying informed about economic events, market trends, and sentiment shifts to make well-informed adjustments to their portfolios.

Conclusion

Effectively monitoring and adjusting a REIT portfolio is a continuous process that demands a balance between routine assessments and the ability to respond to changing market dynamics. Regular check-ins, scheduled portfolio reviews, and leveraging technology for tracking metrics are crucial elements of a comprehensive monitoring strategy. Additionally, the capacity to identify market trends, evaluate economic events, understand market sentiment, and implement adaptive strategies is essential for navigating the dynamic landscape of REIT investments.

Section 3: Rebalancing and Adjusting Your Asset Allocation

In the dynamic landscape of Real Estate Investment Trusts (REITs), the process of monitoring and adjusting extends to fine-tuning your portfolio through effective rebalancing and adjusting asset allocation. In this section, we explore the concept of rebalancing, the importance of assessing portfolio diversification, strategies for adjusting asset allocation based on market conditions, and the implementation of tax-efficient strategies for this purpose.

Fine-Tuning Your Portfolio for Optimal Performance

The goal of fine-tuning a REIT portfolio is to maintain alignment with an investor's financial objectives, risk tolerance, and market conditions. Rebalancing and adjusting asset allocation are critical components of this process, ensuring that the portfolio remains resilient and responsive to changes in the real estate and financial markets.

9.3.1 Understanding the Concept of Rebalancing

- *Definition of Rebalancing*: Rebalancing involves adjusting the weightings of assets in a portfolio to maintain the desired level of risk and return. It is a systematic process that ensures the portfolio stays in line with the investor's original asset allocation strategy.
- *Importance of Rebalancing*: Over time, the performance of different asset classes can vary, leading to shifts in the portfolio's overall risk profile. Rebalancing allows investors to sell overperforming assets and buy underperforming ones, bringing the portfolio back to its target allocation.

9.3.2 Assessing Portfolio Diversification

- *Diversification Benefits*: Diversification is a fundamental principle in investment strategy. Assessing how well a portfolio is diversified involves analyzing the distribution of investments across various asset classes, geographic regions, and property types within the realm of REITs.
- *Risk Management through Diversification*: Diversification helps mitigate risks associated with the performance of specific assets or sectors. A well-diversified REIT portfolio may include exposure to different types of properties

(residential, commercial, healthcare) and diverse geographical locations.

9.3.3 Adjusting Asset Allocation Based on Market Conditions

- *Market Conditions and Allocation*: The real estate market and broader economic conditions can impact the performance of different types of REITs. During periods of economic expansion, certain sectors like commercial REITs might thrive, while in economic downturns, defensive sectors like healthcare REITs might perform better.
- *Dynamic Asset Allocation*: Adjusting asset allocation based on market conditions requires a dynamic approach. Investors may choose to increase exposure to sectors showing potential for growth or reduce exposure to sectors facing headwinds. Regular assessments of market trends inform these decisions.

9.3.4 Tax-Efficient Strategies for Rebalancing

- *Tax Loss Harvesting*: When rebalancing involves selling assets at a loss, investors can use tax loss harvesting strategies to offset gains and minimize tax implications. This involves strategically selling investments that have experienced losses to counterbalance gains elsewhere in the portfolio.
- *Utilizing Tax-Advantaged Accounts*: Rebalancing within tax-advantaged accounts, such as IRAs or 401(k)s, can be more tax-efficient since capital gains taxes are deferred until withdrawals are made. Allocating assets strategically within these accounts can enhance overall tax efficiency.

Implementing tax-efficient strategies when rebalancing and adjusting asset allocation is crucial for optimizing after-tax returns and preserving wealth over the long term.

Conclusion

Rebalancing and adjusting asset allocation are essential elements of managing a successful REIT portfolio. Understanding the concept of rebalancing, assessing portfolio diversification, adapting asset allocation to market conditions, and implementing tax-efficient strategies collectively contribute to the ongoing optimization of the portfolio.

Section 4: Staying Informed about REIT Performance and Market Trends

In the ever-evolving landscape of Real Estate Investment Trusts (REITs), staying informed about performance and market trends is crucial for making informed decisions. This section explores the importance of keeping abreast of critical information and developments, utilizing reliable information sources, identifying key performance indicators for REITs, monitoring economic indicators affecting real estate, and incorporating ongoing education into investment practices.

Keeping Abreast of Critical Information and Developments

9.4.1 Utilizing Reliable Information Sources

- *Financial News Outlets*: Reliable financial news outlets provide up-to-date information on market trends, economic developments, and specific news affecting the real estate sector. Investors should follow reputable sources to stay informed about macroeconomic conditions.

- *REIT-Specific Publications*: Industry-specific publications and reports dedicated to REITs offer in-depth insights into sector-specific trends, company performances, and regulatory changes. Regularly accessing these sources ensures a comprehensive understanding of the REIT market.

9.4.2 Key Performance Indicators for REITs

We will revisit previously discussed indicators.

- *Funds from Operations (FFO)*: FFO is a crucial metric for evaluating the financial performance of REITs. It represents the cash generated by a REIT's operations and is a key indicator of its ability to distribute dividends to shareholders.
- *Net Asset Value (NAV)*: NAV reflects the total value of a REIT's assets minus its liabilities. Monitoring changes in NAV provides insights into the overall financial health and valuation of the REIT.
- *Dividend Yield*: Dividend yield is the annual dividend income as a percentage of the REIT's share price. This metric is essential for income-focused investors seeking consistent returns.

9.4.3 Monitoring Economic Indicators Affecting Real Estate

- *Interest Rates*: Changes in interest rates impact borrowing costs and property valuations, affecting the profitability of REITs. Monitoring interest rate movements helps investors anticipate potential impacts on the real estate market.

- *Housing Market Indicators*: For residential REITs, indicators like home sales, housing starts, and mortgage rates provide insights into the health of the housing market, influencing the performance of residential REITs.

9.4.4 Incorporating Ongoing Education into Investment Practices

- *Industry Conferences and Seminars*: Attending industry conferences and seminars provides opportunities to learn from experts, stay updated on market trends, and gain insights into emerging opportunities or challenges within the REIT sector.
- *Continuous Learning Initiatives*: The dynamic nature of the real estate market requires investors to engage in continuous learning. Reading industry publications, academic research, and participating in online forums contribute to a well-informed investment approach.

Staying informed about REIT performance and market trends goes beyond monitoring financial metrics. Investors should also consider the broader economic landscape, regulatory changes, and industry-specific factors that may impact the real estate market.

Conclusion

Staying informed about REIT performance and market trends is a fundamental aspect of successful REIT investing. Utilizing reliable information sources, understanding key performance indicators, monitoring economic indicators, and incorporating ongoing education into investment practices collectively contribute to informed decision-making.

Investors who prioritize staying well-informed are better positioned to adapt to market changes, identify opportunities, and navigate challenges within the dynamic realm of REIT investments.

Chapter 10: Advanced REIT Strategies

Section 1: Using Options and Derivatives with REITs

As investors gain experience and confidence in navigating the Real Estate Investment Trust (REIT) landscape, the exploration of advanced strategies becomes a natural progression. In this section, we delve into the sophisticated realm of using options and derivatives in REIT investing. Understanding these advanced financial instruments requires a comprehensive examination of options strategies for hedging and income, the application of derivatives in REITs, risk management considerations, and real-world case studies illustrating successful options use in the REIT sector.

Exploring Advanced Financial Instruments in REIT Investing

Investors seeking to maximize returns and manage risk often turn to advanced financial instruments like *options* and *derivatives*. These tools, while more complex than traditional investments, offer unique opportunities for strategic positioning in the market.

10.1.1 Options Strategies for Hedging and Income

- *Hedging Strategies*: Options can be employed as effective hedging tools to protect a REIT portfolio against adverse market movements. *Put* options, for example, can act as insurance, providing the right to sell a security at a predetermined price, mitigating potential losses during market downturns.

- *Income Generation through Covered Calls*: Investors can generate additional income by selling *covered call options* against their existing REIT holdings. This strategy involves selling the right to purchase shares at a predetermined price, providing an additional income stream through the option premium.

10.1.2 Derivatives and Their Application in REITs

- *Interest Rate Swaps*: REITs often face interest rate risks due to their dependency on financing. Interest rate swaps are derivatives that allow REITs to exchange their variable interest rate payments for fixed-rate payments, providing stability in cash flows.
- *Futures Contracts for Property Commodities*: Real estate prices can be volatile, impacting the profitability of REITs. Futures contracts tied to property commodities, such as lumber or steel, enable REITs to lock in prices, mitigating the impact of commodity price fluctuations on their costs.

10.1.3 Risk Management Considerations

- *Leverage and Margin Risks*: While options and derivatives offer strategic advantages, they also introduce leverage and margin risks. Investors must carefully consider the potential for amplified losses when using these instruments and manage their positions accordingly.
- *Market and Liquidity Risks*: Options and derivatives markets can experience rapid movements, and liquidity may vary. Investors need to be aware of market conditions and ensure

that their chosen instruments can be bought or sold at reasonable prices.

10.1.4 Case Studies of Successful Options Use in REITs

- *Risk Mitigation during Economic Downturns*: Case studies can highlight instances where options were successfully used to mitigate risk during economic downturns. For example, during the 2008 financial crisis, some REIT investors utilized put options to protect their portfolios from significant declines.
- *Income Enhancement through Covered Calls*: Examining cases where investors strategically implemented covered calls to enhance income provides valuable insights. Successful examples showcase the potential for generating additional revenue through options strategies.

Conclusion

Exploring advanced strategies involving options and derivatives adds a layer of complexity and sophistication to REIT investing. While these instruments offer unique benefits, they also come with increased risk and complexity. Investors must carefully assess their risk tolerance, market conditions, and financial goals before incorporating advanced strategies into their REIT portfolios.

Section 2: Leveraging and Margin Trading

Real Estate Investment Trusts (REITs) offer investors the opportunity to participate in real estate markets without directly owning physical properties. Leveraging and margin trading are advanced strategies that some investors use to maximize returns. This section delves into the concept of *leverage*, explores the risks and rewards associated with margin trading in REITs, discusses *margin call* considerations, and outlines strategies for prudent leveraging in this unique investment landscape.

10.2.1 Understanding the Concept of Leverage

Leverage Defined: Leverage involves using borrowed funds to increase the size of an investment. In the context of REITs, leverage can amplify returns, potentially enhancing profits when markets are favorable.

Common Leverage Mechanisms: Investors typically leverage their investments through margin accounts, loans, or derivatives. In the case of REITs, margin trading is a common approach. Investors can borrow funds to invest in additional REIT shares beyond what they could afford with their own capital.

Potential for Magnified Returns: The primary allure of leverage is the potential for magnified returns. If the value of the leveraged investment increases, the gains are calculated on the total investment amount (including borrowed funds), leading to a higher percentage return than if the investor had used only their own capital.

Interest Costs: While leverage magnifies potential returns, it also introduces interest costs. Investors leveraging their REIT investments must consider the interest rates associated with borrowed funds. The cost of borrowing can offset gains, particularly in periods of market downturns or when interest rates are high.

10.2.2 Risks and Rewards of Margin Trading in REITs

Rewards

Enhanced Returns: The primary reward of margin trading in REITs is the potential for enhanced returns. By using borrowed funds to increase the size of their investment, investors can benefit from the appreciation of a larger asset base.

Portfolio Diversification: Leverage can also be used to diversify a REIT portfolio. Investors can access a broader range of REITs and market sectors with a smaller initial investment, potentially spreading risk across different real estate segments.

Efficient Capital Deployment: Margin trading allows investors to efficiently deploy their capital. Rather than fully paying for each REIT share in cash, investors can use leverage to increase their exposure without tying up all of their available capital.

Risks

Magnified Losses: While leverage can amplify gains, it also magnifies losses. If the market moves against the investor, the losses incurred on the leveraged portion of the investment can be substantial. This heightened risk is a crucial consideration for those engaging in margin trading.

Interest Costs: Interest costs associated with margin trading can erode profits. If the return on the leveraged investment is not sufficient to cover borrowing costs, investors may find themselves in a position where the overall return on investment is negative.

Market Volatility Exposure: Leveraged positions are particularly sensitive to market volatility. Rapid and unpredictable market movements can result in significant losses, and investors using margin trading must be prepared for the inherent uncertainty of financial markets.

10.2.3 Margin Call Considerations

A Margin Call Defined: One of the critical aspects of margin trading is the concept of a margin call. A margin call occurs when the value of the leveraged investment falls below a certain level, prompting the broker to request additional funds to bring the account back to the required margin.

Forced Liquidation: If an investor fails to meet a margin call, the broker may initiate forced liquidation of assets within the account to cover the outstanding debt. This can result in selling REIT shares at a potentially unfavorable time, crystallizing losses for the investor.

Monitoring Margin Levels: Investors engaging in margin trading must consistently monitor their margin levels and be prepared to inject additional funds into their account if the market moves unfavorably. Diligent risk management is crucial to avoid margin calls and forced liquidation.

10.2.4 Strategies for Prudent Leveraging in REITs

Calculate Risk Tolerance: Before engaging in margin trading, investors should assess their risk tolerance. Understanding how much risk one can comfortably bear is crucial, especially when dealing with leveraged investments that can lead to substantial losses.

Diversify Leveraged Positions: Rather than concentrating leverage on a single REIT or a specific sector, investors may opt to diversify their leveraged positions. Diversification can help mitigate risks associated with the performance of a particular REIT or market segment.

Use Leverage Conservatively: Prudent leveraging involves using borrowed funds conservatively. Instead of maximizing leverage, investors may choose a more moderate approach, allowing for increased exposure while managing potential downsides.

Continuous Monitoring and Risk Management: Investors employing leverage should continuously monitor their positions and implement robust risk management strategies. Regularly assessing the performance of leveraged investments, setting stop-loss orders, and having a clear exit strategy are vital components of prudent leveraging.

Long-Term Investment Perspective: Leveraging in REITs should align with a long-term investment perspective. Short-term market fluctuations may trigger volatility in leveraged positions, but a long-term horizon can provide the necessary time for investments to potentially recover from downturns.

Conclusion

Leveraging and margin trading in REITs can offer the potential for enhanced returns but come with significant risks. Understanding the concept of leverage, evaluating the risks and rewards of margin trading, considering margin call implications, and implementing prudent leveraging strategies are crucial for investors venturing into this advanced territory.

Section 3: International REIT Investing

As investors seek to diversify their portfolios and capitalize on global opportunities, international Real Estate Investment Trusts (REITs) present a compelling avenue. In this section, we explore the nuances of international REIT investing, including the benefits and challenges, considerations for managing currency risks, strategies for researching and selecting international REITs, and the diversification benefits derived from exposure to global real estate markets.

Expanding Opportunities through Global Real Estate Markets

The global real estate market offers a vast array of opportunities for investors looking to broaden their investment horizons. International REITs provide a vehicle for gaining exposure to real estate assets beyond domestic borders, unlocking diverse markets, and potentially enhancing overall portfolio performance.

10.3.1 Benefits and Challenges of International REITs

- *Diversification*: One of the primary benefits of international REITs is diversification. By investing in real estate assets across different countries and regions, investors can reduce their exposure to local market fluctuations and specific economic conditions.
- *Access to Unique Markets*: International REITs provide access to real estate markets with unique characteristics and growth potential that may differ from domestic markets. This allows investors to participate in the development and prosperity of various regions.
- *Global Economic Exposure*: Investing in international REITs exposes investors to the economic conditions of multiple countries. This broad exposure can be advantageous during periods when certain regions outperform others.
- *Challenges*: However, international REIT investing comes with its challenges, including currency risks, differences in

regulatory environments, and potential geopolitical uncertainties.

10.3.2 Currency Risks and Exchange Rate Considerations

- *Impact of Currency Fluctuations*: Investing in international REITs involves exposure to multiple currencies. Changes in exchange rates can impact returns when converted back to the investor's base currency. Understanding and managing currency risks are crucial aspects of international REIT investing.
- *Hedging Strategies*: Investors may choose to implement hedging strategies to mitigate the impact of currency fluctuations. Currency hedging involves using financial instruments to offset potential losses resulting from adverse exchange rate movements.

10.3.3 Researching and Selecting International REITs

- *Market Research and Due Diligence*: Thorough market research and due diligence are essential when considering international REITs. Understanding local real estate markets, economic conditions, and regulatory frameworks is crucial for making informed investment decisions.
- *Management Quality and Track Record*: Assessing the quality of the REIT's management team becomes even more critical when investing internationally. A track record of successfully navigating diverse markets and adapting to local conditions is indicative of a well-managed international REIT.

10.3.4 Diversification Benefits from Global Exposure

- *Geographical and Economic Diversification*: International REITs contribute to geographical and economic diversification. Different regions may experience economic cycles at different times, providing a level of insulation against localized downturns.
- *Sector Diversification*: Investing globally in real estate can also offer sector diversification. Different countries may have varying dominant sectors, such as residential, commercial, or industrial real estate, providing investors exposure to a diverse set of assets.

Conclusion

International REIT investing is a strategic move for investors looking to expand their portfolios and capitalize on global real estate opportunities. While it presents benefits such as diversification and access to unique markets, it requires careful consideration of currency risks, regulatory environments, and thorough due diligence.

Whether through advanced financial instruments, leveraging and margin trading, or international exposure, the overarching goal is to tailor these strategies to align with individual investment objectives and risk tolerances. Advanced REIT strategies, when approached thoughtfully, can complement an investor's broader financial plan and contribute to long-term success.

Section 4: Incorporating REITs into a Comprehensive Investment Strategy

As investors evolve in their journey, integrating Real Estate Investment Trusts (REITs) into a comprehensive investment strategy becomes a key consideration. In this section, we explore the dynamics of seamlessly blending REITs with other asset classes, aligning these investments with overarching financial goals, assessing risk and return profiles across the portfolio, and crafting long-term wealth-building strategies.

Integrating REITs into a Holistic Investment Approach

Incorporating REITs into an investment strategy is more than a tactical decision; it's a strategic move aimed at creating a well-rounded and diversified portfolio. Let's delve into the essential aspects of this integration.

10.4.1 Portfolio Synergy with Other Asset Classes

- *Diversification Benefits*: The primary advantage of integrating REITs lies in diversification. Real estate often exhibits different market behaviors than stocks or bonds, offering a unique set of risk and return characteristics. Combining REITs with other asset classes can contribute to overall portfolio stability.
- *Correlation Analysis*: Investors must conduct correlation analyses to understand how REITs interact with existing holdings. Ideally, assets within a portfolio should have low or negative correlations to mitigate risk during market fluctuations.

10.4.2 Aligning REIT Investments with Overall Financial Goals

- *Income Generation and Capital Appreciation*: REITs can play a dual role in an investment strategy, providing a steady income stream through dividends and potential capital appreciation over time. Aligning these features with an investor's financial goals is crucial for effective integration.
- *Risk Tolerance and Investment Horizon*: Understanding personal risk tolerance and investment horizon remains fundamental. Some investors may prioritize stable income and opt for income-focused REITs, while others with a longer horizon may seek growth-oriented options.

10.4.3 Assessing Risk and Return Profiles Across the Portfolio

- *Risk Assessment*: Combining asset classes involves an in-depth analysis of risk factors. Different assets carry distinct risks, and assessing how these risks interact within the portfolio is critical. Investors need to strike a balance between risk and return, tailoring their portfolio to their risk tolerance.
- *Rebalancing Strategies*: Regular portfolio reviews and rebalancing are essential to maintain the desired risk and return profiles. Reallocating assets based on changing market conditions ensures that the portfolio remains aligned with the investor's goals.

10.4.4 Long-Term Wealth Building Strategies with REITs

- *Compounding Wealth through Dividends*: The compounding effect of reinvesting REIT dividends can significantly contribute to long-term wealth building. Investors may choose to reinvest dividends to acquire additional shares, enhancing their ownership in the underlying real estate assets.

- *Tax-Efficient Wealth Building*: Leveraging tax-efficient strategies, such as holding REITs in tax-advantaged accounts, can enhance wealth-building efficiency. Strategies like tax loss harvesting and mindful asset location contribute to overall tax optimization.

Conclusion

Incorporating REITs into a comprehensive investment strategy requires a thoughtful and strategic approach. Investors should view their portfolio holistically, considering the synergy between asset classes, aligning investments with financial goals, and carefully managing risk and return profiles.

As we conclude the exploration of advanced REIT strategies, it is crucial to emphasize that each investor's journey is unique. Advanced strategies, including leveraging, international exposure, and integration into a comprehensive investment plan, should be undertaken with a deep understanding of individual financial circumstances and risk tolerance.

The journey through REIT investing is dynamic, and as market conditions, economic landscapes, and personal financial goals evolve, investors must stay informed, adapt their strategies, and continue the pursuit of long-term wealth creation. The integration of REITs into a broader investment strategy is not just about optimizing returns; it's about crafting a resilient and dynamic financial plan that aligns with an investor's vision for the future.

Conclusion: The Future of REIT Investing

Section 1: Emerging Trends in the REIT Market

As we navigate the conclusion of this journey into REIT investing, it's imperative to cast our gaze forward, examining the emerging trends that will shape the future of this dynamic market.

Technology Integration

The incorporation of technology into the real estate sector has been transformative, and the same holds true for REITs. The adoption of PropTech (Property Technology) is becoming a cornerstone in REIT operations.

- *Role of Proptech in REIT Operations*: Proptech platforms streamline various aspects of property management, from tenant interactions to maintenance scheduling. REITs leveraging these technologies gain efficiency, reducing operational costs and enhancing tenant satisfaction.
- *Smart Buildings and the Internet of Things (IoT)*: Smart building technologies, powered by the Internet of Things, are reshaping the real estate landscape. From energy-efficient systems to enhanced security protocols, these innovations are not only improving property performance but also influencing investment decisions.
- *Tech-driven Innovations in Property Management*: Automation, artificial intelligence, and data analytics are revolutionizing property management. Predictive

maintenance, energy optimization, and data-driven decision-making are becoming standard practices, optimizing the overall performance of REIT portfolios.

1.2 Sustainable and ESG Investing

Environmental, Social, and Governance (ESG) considerations are increasingly becoming integral to investment decisions. The REIT market is no exception, with a growing emphasis on sustainable and responsible practices.

- *Impact of ESG Criteria*: Investors are recognizing the long-term benefits of integrating ESG criteria into investment strategies. REITs aligning with these principles are not only contributing to broader sustainability goals but are also mitigating risks associated with environmental and social issues.
- *Growing Demand for Green Buildings*: The demand for environmentally sustainable buildings is on the rise. REITs investing in green technologies and environmentally friendly practices are poised to attract environmentally-conscious tenants, thereby enhancing property value and marketability.
- *ESG Reporting and Accountability in REITs*: Transparent reporting on ESG metrics is becoming a standard practice for REITs. Investors are increasingly valuing companies that exhibit a commitment to ethical practices, social responsibility, and effective governance.

1.3 Evolving Property Types

The landscape of real estate is dynamic, and so is the composition of REIT portfolios. Non-traditional property types are gaining prominence, reflecting the evolving needs and preferences of investors and tenants alike.

- *Trends in Non-traditional REIT Investments*: REITs are diversifying into non-traditional asset classes, such as data centers, cell towers, and logistics centers. These properties often demonstrate resilience and attractive growth prospects, aligning with the demands of the modern economy.
- *Adapting to Changing Consumer Behaviors*: The retail landscape within REITs is adapting to changing consumer behaviors. E-commerce trends, for instance, are reshaping the demand for warehousing and distribution centers. REITs agile enough to respond to these shifts are well-positioned for sustained success.

Conclusion

The future of REIT investing is intricately woven with technological advancements, sustainable practices, and an agile approach to evolving property types. Investors venturing into the REIT market must not only understand the historical context and current dynamics but also remain attuned to these emerging trends.

As we anticipate the future, the resilience of REITs lies not just in the bricks and mortar but in their adaptability to a dynamic market landscape. The integration of technology, commitment to sustainable practices, and a strategic approach to property types will undoubtedly shape the success stories of REITs in the years to come. As you embark on your REIT investment journey, may you find success in navigating the ever-evolving landscape of real estate investment trusts.

Section 2: Long-Term Prospects for REIT

Investors

Investing in Real Estate Investment Trusts (REITs) demands a forward-looking perspective. Understanding the long-term prospects involves a comprehensive analysis of macro-economic factors, the regulatory landscape, and the role of technological advancements in shaping the future of REIT investments.

Macro-Economic Factors

2.1.1 Interest Rate Trends and Their Impact

Interest rates play a pivotal role in the real estate market, influencing property values, financing costs, and investor behavior. A nuanced understanding of interest rate trends is crucial for REIT investors planning for the long term.

Historically, real estate and interest rates share an inverse relationship. As interest rates rise, borrowing becomes more expensive, potentially dampening property values. However, this relationship is complex, as rising rates may also indicate a strong economy, positively impacting property demand. Long-term REIT investors must monitor interest rate trends, considering the broader economic context, to make informed investment decisions.

2.1.2 Demographic Shifts and Housing Markets

Demographic trends are key determinants of real estate demand. The aging population, urbanization, and shifts in household structures all influence housing markets. Understanding these demographic dynamics is vital for assessing the long-term viability of residential REITs.

For instance, an aging population often correlates with increased demand for senior housing and healthcare facilities. On the other hand, millennials entering the housing market may drive demand for rental properties and urban living spaces. Long-term REIT investors need to align their portfolios with these demographic shifts to capitalize on emerging opportunities.

2.1.3 Global Economic Influences on Real Estate Markets

Real estate is interconnected with global economic trends. The rise of emerging markets, global trade dynamics, and geopolitical factors all contribute to the performance of real estate assets. Long-term REIT investors must broaden their scope to understand how global economic influences can impact their portfolios.

Global economic growth can drive demand for commercial properties, while economic downturns may impact the performance of certain sectors. Diversification across geographical regions and staying attuned to global economic trends are essential strategies for long-term REIT investors.

2.2 Regulatory Landscape

2.2.1 Changes in Tax Laws Affecting REITs

Tax laws play a pivotal role in shaping the profitability of REIT investments. Long-term investors must stay abreast of changes in tax regulations that could impact the attractiveness of REITs as an investment vehicle.

Recent tax reforms may introduce new considerations, such as alterations in dividend taxation or changes in pass-through status for

REITs. Regular updates on tax laws and consultation with tax professionals are essential for navigating the evolving tax landscape.

2.2.2 Regulatory Environment and Compliance

REITs operate within a regulatory framework that influences their operations, reporting requirements, and compliance standards. Changes in these regulations can have profound effects on REITs' ability to raise capital, manage portfolios, and distribute returns to investors.

Investors with a long-term horizon need to assess how changes in the regulatory environment may impact the specific REITs in their portfolios. Adherence to compliance standards is critical for the sustainable growth and success of REITs over time.

2.2.3 Policy Implications on Real Estate Investment

Government policies related to infrastructure development, zoning laws, and housing initiatives can significantly impact real estate markets. Long-term REIT investors should factor in the potential effects of government policies on the sectors in which their REITs operate.

For instance, policies promoting sustainable development or incentivizing affordable housing may present opportunities for certain types of REITs. Conversely, regulatory measures restricting real estate development may pose challenges. An in-depth analysis of policy implications is integral to forecasting the long-term prospects of REIT investments.

Technological Advancements

2.3.1 Integration of PropTech in Real Estate

The integration of Property Technology (PropTech) is reshaping how real estate is managed and operated. For long-term REIT investors, understanding and leveraging PropTech innovations are essential for maintaining a competitive edge.

PropTech encompasses a range of technologies, from smart building management systems to virtual property tours. REITs that embrace and integrate PropTech can enhance property efficiency, reduce costs, and provide a more attractive offering to tenants.

2.3.2 AI and Big Data in Property Analysis

Artificial Intelligence (AI) and Big Data analytics are revolutionizing property analysis. Long-term REIT investors should be cognizant of the potential of AI and Big Data in predicting market trends, optimizing property performance, and identifying lucrative investment opportunities.

Machine learning algorithms can analyze vast datasets to forecast market trends and assess property value fluctuations. REITs that incorporate these technologies into their strategies can gain a competitive advantage in the long run.

2.3.3 Potential Disruptions and Innovations

Technological advancements may also bring disruptive innovations to the real estate market. Concepts like blockchain, which facilitate transparent and secure transactions, or the use of 3D printing in construction, have the potential to reshape the industry.

Long-term REIT investors need to stay vigilant about emerging technologies that could introduce both risks and opportunities. Being adaptable to technological disruptions is crucial for sustained success in the ever-evolving real estate landscape.

Conclusion

In contemplating the long-term prospects for REIT investors, a holistic view is imperative. The macro-economic environment, regulatory landscape, and technological advancements collectively shape the trajectory of REIT investments. Investors with a foresighted approach, grounded in an understanding of these multifaceted factors, are better positioned to navigate the challenges and capitalize on the opportunities that the future holds for REITs. As the real estate market continues to evolve, the adage of "knowledge is power" becomes increasingly relevant for those embarking on or continuing their journey in the realm of REIT investing.

Section 3: Final Thoughts and Encouragement for Beginners

Embarking on the journey of Real Estate Investment Trust (REIT) investing is a significant step towards building wealth and securing financial well-being. As beginners navigate the complexities of the real estate market through the REIT lens, it's crucial to reflect on the journey, commit to ongoing learning, and find encouragement for future endeavors.

Reflection on the Journey

3.1.1 Progress and Learning for Novice Investors

For novice investors, the journey into REIT investing is marked by progress and continuous learning. Reflecting on the initial steps, such as defining investment goals and understanding risk tolerance, helps appreciate the growth achieved. Recognizing the learning curve and the ability to decipher complex real estate dynamics instills confidence in the investment journey.

3.1.2 Celebrating Achievements and Lessons Learned

Celebrating achievements, regardless of their scale, is vital for beginners. From successfully selecting the first REIT to understanding and interpreting financial metrics, each milestone contributes to the investor's knowledge and experience. Equally important is acknowledging lessons learned from any challenges faced, turning setbacks into opportunities for growth.

3.1.3 Navigating Challenges in REIT Investing

Challenges are inherent in any investment journey, and REIT investing is no exception. Whether dealing with market volatility, adjusting to economic changes, or reassessing portfolio strategies, recognizing challenges as stepping stones to growth is crucial. Navigating challenges fosters resilience and sharpens the skills needed for long-term success in the world of REITs.

Ongoing Learning and Adaptation

3.2.1 Commitment to Lifelong Learning in Real Estate

A commitment to lifelong learning is the cornerstone of success in real estate investing. Beginners should view their initial foray into REITs as the beginning of an educational journey. Staying informed about market trends, regulatory changes, and advancements in real estate technology is essential for making informed decisions.

3.2.2 Staying Informed about Market Developments

Real estate markets are dynamic, influenced by economic, social, and technological shifts. Staying informed about these developments empowers investors to make proactive decisions. Utilizing reputable sources, attending industry events, and engaging with experienced investors contribute to a well-rounded understanding of the ever-evolving real estate landscape.

3.2.3 Leveraging Resources for Continued Growth

As beginners progress, leveraging resources becomes crucial. From financial experts and mentors to online forums and educational platforms, there is a wealth of resources available. Engaging with these resources facilitates continuous growth and ensures that investors are equipped to navigate the complexities of REIT investing.

3.3 Encouragement for Future Endeavors

3.3.1 Embracing the Journey of Wealth Building

The journey of wealth building through REIT investing is a marathon, not a sprint. Encouragement lies in embracing the incremental growth achieved over time. Consistent and disciplined investment practices, coupled with a focus on long-term goals, position beginners to create sustainable wealth through their REIT portfolios.

3.3.2 Building Confidence in Financial Decision-Making

Confidence in financial decision-making is nurtured through knowledge and experience. Beginners should take pride in their ability to make informed choices, be it in selecting specific REITs, adjusting portfolio allocations, or responding to market changes. Confidence builds with each successful decision, contributing to a more resilient and competent investor.

3.3.3 Inspiring Continued Exploration in Real Estate Investing

The world of real estate investing is vast and multifaceted. Encouraging beginners to explore different facets, whether by diversifying across REIT types or considering advanced strategies, inspires a sense of curiosity and entrepreneurship. The evolving nature of the real estate market provides ample opportunities for those willing to explore and adapt.

Conclusion

In conclusion, the final thoughts for beginners in REIT investing revolve around reflection, ongoing learning, and encouragement. The journey is a continuous process of growth, and every challenge is an opportunity to refine skills and strategies. By committing to lifelong learning, staying informed, and embracing the journey of wealth building, beginners can navigate the complexities of REIT investing with confidence and enthusiasm. The real estate market offers a canvas for financial creativity, and every investor has the potential to paint a successful picture through strategic and informed decisions.

Good luck.

Check out WWW.JIMPELLERIN.COM[1] for more articles on Real Estate Investing.

1. http://WWW.JIMPELLERIN.COM

About The Author

JIM PELLERIN started real estate investing over twenty years ago. Since then, he has bought and sold millions of dollars of real estate. He began by purchasing and renting out duplexes. Recently he has added Lease Options to his strategy. He is currently acquiring two to four Lease Option properties a month. He has implemented many unique funding strategies that have allowed him to continue implementing his strategy and continue building his sizable portfolio.

As part of his education, he has attended numerous seminars on real estate investing, project management, property management, financing, renovations, motivation, time management, and many more. He has also read over 500 books on similar topics.

This book blends his experience and the knowledge he has gained through his investments and studies.

Visit his author page to discover my other publications: books2read.com/JimPellerin[1]

1. https://books2read.com/JimPellerin

Other Books By Jim Pellerin

Real Estate Investing: Strategies – The Secret to Financial Independence with Real Estate

books2read.com/strategies[1]

1. https://books2read.com/strategies

Real Estate Investing with Lease Options – How to Invest with No Money Down

books2read.com/Lease-Options[2]

2. https://books2read.com/Lease-Options

Invest NOW – The Passive Approach to Winning with Real Estate

books2read.com/investnow[3]

3. https://books2read.com/investnow

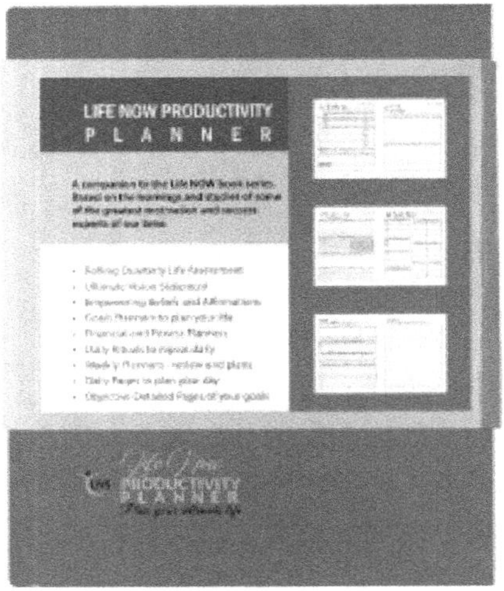

books2read.com/JimPellerin[4]

4. https://books2read.com/JimPellerin

Don't miss out!

Visit the website below and you can sign up to receive emails whenever Jim Pellerin publishes a new book. There's no charge and no obligation.

https://books2read.com/r/B-A-WGIX-IOHYC

BOOKS 2 READ

Connecting independent readers to independent writers.

Did you love *Mastering REIT Investments - A Comprehensive Guide to Wealth Building*? Then you should read *Real Estate Investing Strategies: The Secret to Financial Independence with Real Estate*[5] by Jim Pellerin!

[6]

The mechanics of Real Estate Investing is simple: Buy a house and do something with it. Fix it and rent it, or just sell it. Sounds simple, doesn't it? Yet only a small percentage of us have enough courage to go out and take advantage of the opportunities that are available to us. Real Estate Investing can be more promising than stocks, bonds, and various other securities because of the higher rates of return.

In this book, I show you how to get started by describing the different types of skills you need, by showing you how to take control of your personal and financial situation, and by helping you decide what

5. https://books2read.com/u/m2QyNG

6. https://books2read.com/u/m2QyNG

type of real estate investing you want to get involved in. I also show you how to find properties, how to analyze them, and how to make an offer that makes sense. And finally, I describe what you need to do to manage your investment and ultimately how to sell your investment for the most profit.

I have been involved in real estate investing for over 20 years. I have yet to find a book that focuses on the investor and the overall process. Sure, there are lots of books on fix and flips, buy, rent and hold, rent to own, etc. However, I haven't found any good books on how to really get started in the real estate investing process from a practical viewpoint. The technical aspects of real estate investing are really quite easy. But if it's so easy, then why isn't everyone doing it?

This book is for people who are serious about getting started in real estate investing and who want to join the 5% of those who actually take action and invest. This book provides a strategic approach with the tried and tested methods and principles that have helped others make millions in real estate.

Read more at www.jimpellerin.com.

Also by Jim Pellerin

Life Now

Invest Now - The Passive Approach to Winning at Real Estate

Real Estate Investing

Real Estate Investing Strategies: The Secret to Financial Independence with Real Estate

Real Estate Investing with Lease Options - Investing in Real Estate with No Money Down

Mastering REIT Investments - A Comprehensive Guide to Wealth Building

The Ultimate Beginners Guide to Real Estate Investing

The 98 Best Real Estate Investing Strategies

The Ultimate Beginners Guide to Wholesale Real Estate Investing

The Ultimate Beginners Guide to Rental Real Estate Investing

The Ultimate Beginners Guide to Fix and Flip Real Estate Investing

The Ultimate Beginners Guide to Private Equity Real Estate Investing

Ultimate Beginners Guide to Real Estate Investing Financing

Building Wealth Through Real Estate - A Beginners Retirement Guide

The Ultimate Guide to Marketing for Real Estate Investors

Unleashing Wealth: A Guide to BRRRR Real Estate Investing

Watch for more at www.jimpellerin.com.

About the Author

Jim Pellerin has been investing in Real Estate for over 25 years. During that time, he has conducted over $30M worth of real estate transactions.

He was the founder of several Real Estate businesses with the latest, Peller Media, focusing on providing digital marketing services for real estate professionals such as real estate agents and mortgage brokers and investors.

He has read over 700 books on subjects such as real estate investing, self development, education, cognitive psychology, marketing and sales.

He has a degree in Computer Science which he received from the University of New Brunswick in Fredericton, New Brunswick, Canada.

Read more at www.jimpellerin.com.

www.ingramcontent.com/pod-product-compliance
Lightning Source LLC
LaVergne TN
LVHW022041200926
848481LV00003B/743
* 9 7 9 8 2 2 4 3 7 6 4 4 5 *